No Longer Alone

Joan Winmill Brown

SPECIAL CRUSADE EDITION
Published for the
Billy Graham Evangelistic Association
Published by
World Wide Publications
1303 Hennepin Avenue
Minneapolis, Minnesota 55403

Scripture quotations not otherwise identified are from the King James Version of
the Bible.

Scripture quotations identified LB are from The Living Bible, Copyright © 1971 by
Tyndale House Publishers, Wheaton, Illinois 60187. All rights reserved.

The poem "Loneliness" from *The Unwanted Statue and Other Poems* by Sarah
Churchill is used by permission of Leslie Frewin Publishers Limited, London.

Library of Congress Cataloging in Publication Data

Brown, Joan Winmill.
   No longer alone.

   1. Brown, Joan Winmill.   2. Conversion. I. Title.
PN2287.B719A34   791´.092´4[B]   75-23195
ISBN 0-89066-010-7

1

I looked around the furnished London apartment and saw a hodgepodge of other people's mistakes—furniture that had no character. There were no signs of a woman's touch here, for I had given up caring. This was just a place to sleep and eat and sometimes, even amongst the terrible emptiness and loneliness, a refuge. I did not have to face people here. No "act" was necessary. The characterless chairs and walls required nothing of me, and I knew they would not talk behind my back.

But the nights were interminable, and my imagination would conjure up all kinds of conversations people were having about me. "My dear, she's obviously neurotic—a hypochondriac to boot. Look at her record—two nervous breakdowns. Who would want to employ her? She might let the show down; and then where would you be?"

I remembered I had once let the show down when the first breakdown was coming on. My speech had started to slur, and I panicked every time I had to go onstage or before a camera, for fear of forgetting my lines. Several times I experienced that overwhelming fear—stage fright—when it seemed the audience became some dark monster waiting to pounce. I floundered for my lines and drew a terrifying blank. Somehow I would hear the whispered cue from the wings, and drawing myself together, I would summon all the courage I had and proceed with the scene.

I was playing the part of a bright, American millionairess who was engaged to an Earl's son in *The Chiltern Hundreds,* a play by

William Douglas Home. The part was based on Kathleen Kennedy, sister to Bobby and Jack Kennedy. The play ran for two years in London, and that should have been the happiest time of my life. Instead, it was marred by fears, doubts, and a feeling of never quite belonging anywhere I went. My health suffered, and when I collapsed from sheer exhaustion, the author of the play sent me to his family home in Scotland to recuperate. The thought of letting the cast down had haunted me ever since. Now here I was again, sinking rapidly, and there seemed to be no way out.

"Dear God, please help me!"

In the darkness of that lonely apartment I realized I had offered a prayer—after so long!

My career as an actress had spanned eight years. It had included roles in a number of films, in addition to many stage parts and television appearances. Yet my life at twenty-seven was, putting it mildly, a mess. My health was broken. I could not work properly, and nothing seemed worthwhile. Apart from the complexity of my life, I knew I was on the verge of a third breakdown. Life held nothing for me. That morning I had read of an actress friend who had committed suicide. I envied her. *How* I envied her! Her battles were over; mine were still going on, and I didn't have the energy or desire to strive any more.

"Oh, if only I could escape! I've got to get out of this frightening entanglement. Dear God, please help me! I remember when I prayed to You as a child, You were very close to me. Now I seem to have gone so far from You. When I see a church I want to go in and kneel and cry my heart out. But I'm afraid. Not of You, but of people. Why? Is it because I have not lived as I should, and I wonder what they are thinking? When I used to recite the Psalms, there was always the consciousness of whether I was being watched to see if I knew the words. The atmosphere of that church is vivid in my memory, for in spite of feeling unworthy, there was the beauty of worshiping You. I miss that so desperately. Doors seem to be shutting in my life, and there doesn't seem to be much hope left. The dream I once had has faded, and I'm left with an emptiness it seems can never be filled."

I walked over to the window. I had often stood there, watching the large tree and envying it. There seemed to be a peace about it, even though it was rooted and could not move. I dreaded being tied down. The branches swayed in the wind. I had watched the leaves fall that winter, leaving a stark, bare outline. The tree seemed to be sleeping, oblivious of all that had happened around it. Spring would come and inevitably the buds would burst forth into leaves once more. The cycle was comforting to think about, and yet I did not see how there could be any new beginnings or bursting forth for me. I wished I could shed all the mistakes of my life and start again, but somehow it seemed too late. Peace, that was all I really desired now—to be able to turn off the thoughts that never seemed to give me rest. If only one had a thermostat in one's head which automatically switched off when things became unbearable!

So many friends from school days envied me, for they saw only the glamorous side to my career, not the terrifying heartache and feeling of utter dejection. Why? What had brought me to this place where I no longer had the desire to live? I looked down at the street beneath and wondered about jumping, but then it was only four stories up. "Anyway," I thought, ironically, "I've always been deathly afraid of heights!"

The gas oven looked more and more inviting. I could just turn it on, open the oven door, put a soft pillow on it, rest my head, and sink into a deep, eternal sleep. That is what my friend had done only yesterday.

The telephone rang in the darkness of the apartment.

A battle ensued.

"I can't face anyone! Just to try to act as if there is nothing wrong...."

Again the phone rang, and finally I summoned all the energy I had and picked up the receiver.

"Hello," I said, in a bright and brittle voice.

"Hello, Joan," responded a resonant male voice. "This is John Mercer. Remember we met through my cousin Joy?"

"Why yes, of course, how are you?"

"Fine! Saw you on BBC TV last night and was wondering if you would have dinner with my wife and me next week. We've got some reserved tickets to see Billy Graham and thought we would get up a party to go see him. Might be fun!"

Immediately I began to act.

"Why yes! I've seen the advertising, and it would be a lark to hear what this American has come to tell the British about religion."

We made a date, and after a few more frivolous nuances, I hung up.

I wasn't about to let anyone know that as soon as I had seen the advertising for Billy Graham's meetings I had wanted to go. It seemed that every double-decker bus in London carried the news of his crusade on their sides. But nothing was going to drag that confession of a longing to hear what he had to say out of me, and nothing would expose the need that was deep within me.

Suddenly it seemed as if someone, or something, had stopped me short. That telephone call. Was it God's way of answering my prayer? Surely He doesn't work that quickly. I brushed the thought aside and contemplated anew the gloom around me.

My mind began remembering, remembering incidents of the past—as far back as my childhood—that had brought me to the frightening and lonely existence that now was my life.

Until I was four years old my life was a normal one, except that my mother loved to move, and we had three homes from the time of my birth.

My father traveled in his work, but my mother was able to give me a sense of security. She was a gentle, fun-loving person, who had had to face a heartbreaking separation from my father shortly after my birth. He was sent to a sanitarium for many months, because he developed tuberculosis while living in the mud trenches of World War I. Mother would rise above difficulties with a great sense of humor and meet the challenges as they came. I was often bundled into our car and taken for unknown adventures. Mother was the most beautiful person in my world.

Father was, as far as I was concerned, a giant among men. When he was home the house seemed to generate a boundless peace, and the happiness of my parents overflowed to everyone. As I grew taller my giant father turned out to be what is considered rather short in stature, but he still remained a giant in his loving concern for others. This trait brought about his death years later while trying to save the life of a neighbor.

The first crisis in my life came when I was four years old and visiting my grandmother's house near Wimbledon. Nowadays her house might be called a Victorian monstrosity, but for me it had a personality all of its own. The long corridors, which led to rooms filled with many intriguing objects, were great places to run and imagine all kinds of games. My grandparents' dog, Mick, took part in all my escapades and became many different "people" to me.

The trauma occurred when I saw my mother's suitcase by the front door, and she was dressed to leave.

"Why can't I come with you?" I cried as I clung to her desperately.

"Joan, I have to go somewhere that I can't take you now. It's just for a few days, then Nanny (my name for grandmother) will bring you to me, and I'll have a surprise for you!"

My mother had left me before. But for some reason, this time I cried inconsolably as I watched her walk out of the kitchen and up the three steps which led to the long hall and the colored-glass-paned front door. She picked up the suitcase, opened the door, and was gone from me. The finality of that scene has lived with me all my life.

As is the usual case with young children when their mother leaves, eventually I was distracted and once more went back to playing in my make-believe world with Mick.

But the suitcase still worried me, and I wondered where she could possibly be going that I couldn't go.

A few days later my grandmother told me we were going to my Aunt Hilda's house. (She was my mother's sister.) My mother was there and she would have my surprise.

I was so excited. It would mean riding on the red double-decker bus, and I could look out of the window and see all kinds of interesting happenings. I hugged Mick and told him we would be back soon and I would share my big surprise, whatever it was, with him.

Finally we got to our stop and alighted breathlessly from the bus. The walk to the house seemed unending, too, and I chattered incessantly to my grandmother. She was as excited as I was, and her kind, work-worn hand in mine kept pressing with excitement.

It was a beautiful morning. As we rounded the corner that led to my aunt's house, I thought my heart would burst at the thought of seeing my mother.

We were at the gate and I waited patiently for Grandmother to unlatch it. She hesitated. Then I looked up and saw her face.

It was suddenly drawn and white, and she did not look like the happy grandmother with whom I had traveled. She had seen the curtains drawn shut in all the windows of the house. This was unusual. My aunt loved the sunlight, and her house always shone inside and out.

I was told to play in the garden while Nanny went inside. As I ran up and down in the garden a little impatiently, I was oblivious of the terrible meaning of the drawn curtains.

My mother was dead. My beautiful, fun-loving mother, who had been my security, had died in childbirth. The baby, who was to have been the "surprise," was dead also.

She had not wanted to go to a hospital, but instead had decided to have the baby at my aunt's home, not dreaming there would be the complication of toxemia. The doctor had battled to save her and the baby, but had lost.

For some time I was not told of her death, only that she had had to go away. Then gradually, as I got over the shock of her absence, I was told she was in the hospital. I missed her and was always asking when she was coming back. This must have been a terrible time for my father and my grandparents, as they tried to shield me from the truth.

One day, I remember so vividly, I was sitting on the hard-backed Windsor chair in my grandmother's kitchen, crying for my mother. My father took me on his knee and told me she had died.

Died? I couldn't even comprehend the finality of that word.

"Yes," Daddy said, "she died of pneumonia and has gone to heaven."

Pneumonia? I thought, *That must be the worst illness you could possibly get, for it has killed my mother. But she promised me I could be with her, and now I can't go to see her.*

My father told me that one day we would see her again, but not for a while. All I could feel was that my mother had broken her promise to me, and I sobbed at the thought of this.

He could not bring himself to tell me the truth that she had died in childbirth, for a child of four must not know of these things. In those days childbirth was not discussed with children.

A year later, while traveling on a train with my grandmother, I learned how my mother had really died. Nanny started talking to the stranger opposite, and not finding the conversation very interesting, I sat looking out of the window watching the houses go by and conjuring up all kinds of stories about the occupants. The little row houses clustered so closely together, although of exactly the same architecture, had personalities of their own, depending on who lived in them. Some were so neat, others so higgledy-piggledy with all kinds of junk piled in the back gardens. Others had interesting cats and dogs that kept my attention.

I was brought back to reality by the stranger asking about my mother. My grandmother glanced at me to see if I were listening, but I still looked out of the window. However, I watched them in the reflection.

Quietly Grandmother said, "She died in childbirth. The baby died too—a little boy. Joan believes she died of pneumonia, but actually it was childbirth."

Childbirth, I remember thinking, *why it must be worse than pneumonia,* and a fear of that word came over me which was to stay with me through the years.

3

After my mother's death, my grandparents' house now became home for my father and me. Some of our furniture was brought there, and I would sit alone in the living room remembering times when Mother had sat in the same chairs, or dusted the breakfront, and then opened the glass doors to get a book to read to me.

My grandfather—"Fader" as I called him, because when I was very small I could not pronounce the *th* properly—was a real character. He was twenty years older than my grandmother and was waited on "hand and foot" by her.

The company of lawyers with which he was associated had gone bankrupt, leaving him with very little money and just a small government pension. But to talk to him you would never have known it. He had an aristocratic air about him, even when he sat around the house in his old clothes. His favorite outfit was topped by an old cap with the peak cut off. This intrigued me, and I was told he wore it "to keep the drafts off."

He had one best outfit he kept for his monthly jaunt into Wimbledon. I would watch him get dressed and wonder if he were going to London to see the King—such preparations would go into these outings. His suit would be pressed and brushed by my grandmother. His shoes would be shined to a high polish. He would come down the stairs looking like a very distinguished gentleman. When he donned his black overcoat with the velvet collar, placed his hat carefully at a jaunty angle, and reached for his black, silver-topped cane in the hallstand, I was sure he could pass for a duke.

His white hair and bushy mustache made him look rather like Albert Schweitzer. Surely I had the *most* distinguished grandfather and he was going on such an important mission! It was kept secret from me for a while until finally my grandmother told me in hushed tones, "He goes to pay the rent!" Their Victorian upbringing deemed that one did not discuss money matters with a child.

Fader did not believe in God. He would sit and argue that when you were dead you were dead. There was no heaven and no hell and he couldn't see that God has been too good to *him*. "Not that I believe in Him, mind," he would say.

When my grandfather died, it seemed so very final. I did not feel as if I would ever see him again, for I never heard Fader say anything good about the Lord right up until the time of his death. On the night he died, I remember thinking how very sad it was for someone to have gone through life without wanting to go to heaven. I cannot judge, for I know the love of God is so much greater than we can comprehend. If in some quiet moment he had asked the Lord to receive him—even a second before he passed away—then one of the joys of heaven for me will be to see him there.

Nanny was a gentle person. Always working. Always there when you needed consoling. She was married at a very young age to my demanding grandfather and bore two daughters. There were no modern labor-saving appliances for her. The vacuum had only just been invented and was much too expensive. Her washing machine was a boiler in the kitchen where every Monday, come what may, she did the week's washing. Tuesday was always spent ironing with flatirons heated over the fire.

But Saturday was her big day! For years our routine on that day was as follows: After lunch, which always ended with a suet pudding and treacle ("to keep colds away"), my father would head for the football match; my grandfather would nap by the fire; but Nanny and I would head for the cinema—rain or shine!

We would sit in the "one and nines" (one shilling, nine pence seats), armed with bags of sweets, and be taken out of our everyday world into a fantasy one.

With my fifth birthday came the advent of school and all its complications. A teacher would call in the mornings to walk to school with me. It seemed miles to a five-year-old.

One morning after Nanny had called me, I got out of bed in my usual unwilling way (I have always been a night owl and still am!). I remembered it was a Wednesday, a special day! "Tiger Tim" comic was delivered with the morning newspaper. It was my favorite and the anticipation of it enabled me to wash and dress quickly and come bounding down the stairs. When I burst into the kitchen to ask my grandmother where it was, she could only make strange sounds and try to make me understand by her hands. I thought she was being funny and I made strange noises back at her.

What I did not know was that my dear Nanny was on the verge of a nervous breakdown. The shock of my mother's death had finally caught up with her. Because of this, I was told that I would have to live with my Aunt Hilda and Uncle Hector in Sutton.

I liked going there for visits for I had fun with my cousin Audrey, who was just a year old. But for a regular diet, I was not sure. You see, the whole routine was different. My aunt and uncle were very orderly people and had a strict routine. Nanny, on the other hand, could be twisted around my little finger, to say nothing of my grandfather. With Nanny, bedtime was when I felt tired; and I could read until all hours, with all kinds of candy hidden under the mattress—but not so with Aunt Hilda!

My poor aunt was now saddled with a very unpredictable five-year-old, just at a time when she had enough to handle with a year-old baby. Luckily, she had a nurse to help her for a while. The move meant changing schools too, and if anyone had said then that the Lord knew what He was doing with my life, I could not have believed it. In changing schools, I was to encounter someone who had a great influence on me. It was the Headmistress who taught the Scriptures and was a very dedicated person.

Gradually I got used to the strict routine, but I was always glad when Friday nights came, for after my grandmother recovered, my father would collect me and I would spend the weekend with them. Imagine how relieved my aunt and uncle were!

I enjoyed my school—St. Hilda's School. It was small, but the teachers were wonderful. Miss Cashmore, my class teacher, also taught elocution and from her I got my first encouragement to be an actress. I would enter local drama festivals and won several medals for giving readings. Then the school plays were always a highlight in my life.

My school required church attendance, and there I would sit with the Headmistress. I always looked forward to that. It was the Church of England in Carshalton, a very beautiful, old parish church, nestled by a lovely pond with swans on it. The atmosphere of the church was slightly overwhelming to me when I first started attending and the Vicar seemed to be someone who had really been set apart from all of us mortals. He was an elderly, austere man and when he got up into the pulpit to preach—I listened. I listened—but I did not understand what he was talking about. I knew it was important, but as to it relating to me, it went right above my head. Miss Godfrey, the Headmistress, had the great gift of being able to make the Bible come alive, and so I relied on her to answer all my questions.

There were the nativity plays every Christmas that delighted me. One year my big role was Violante in a beautiful little play in which I had to sing Christina Rossetti's poem, "Mid-Winter":

> What can I give Him, poor as I am?
> If I were a shepherd I would bring a lamb.
> If I were a wise man I would play my part,
> What can I give Him?
> I'll give Him my heart.

It has always been a favorite of mine. I only wish that the last line had had a deeper effect on me.

Then came another trauma for me when I was ten years old. One weekend, as my father was driving me to my grandmother's, he said he had some news for me. My Aunt Hilda was going to have another baby and wouldn't be able to take care of me any longer. Once again the birth of a baby was to change the course of my life and I did not look forward to the arrival one bit.

Daddy told me he had found a lady who was willing to look after me. She lived near my aunt so I could still see my cousin Audrey and play over there often. Also I could still go to St. Hilda's School. At least, during the holidays, I could stay with Nanny and travel with my father sometimes. I lived always in a world of looking forward to my father coming to pick me up to take me with him.

The house I went to live in was perhaps one of the most beautiful in Carshalton. It was surrounded by a very high brick wall which secluded it completely from the outside world. One passed through the tall white gate into a beautiful garden where old trees and flowers surrounded a lush, green lawn. The front door with the ornate brass knocker opened to reveal an elegance of another world. The house was built in the late eighteenth century and had all the grace of the Georgian period. The rooms were lofty, with large windows overlooking the garden, and were furnished with antiques and tasteful furniture. In the living room was the largest grand piano I had ever seen.

The owners of the house were a very kind couple who did not have children of their own. They tried very hard to win me over. I had a lovely room. Everything was done to make me happy, but I never felt that I belonged. Once again, it was a different way of life, a different routine, and I would cry myself to sleep so many nights.

I especially remember one day at the house when I sat by the window in my room, sorting horse chestnuts and displaying them on the windowsill. I overheard the lady tell my father it would be better if he did not visit me for a while as I was always upset when he left. That did it, and the thought of not seeing him for a long time triggered off all the old fears. Since Daddy also didn't agree with her, a few weeks later I went to live with someone else.

In the next house there was a daughter a little older than I, so I felt I would not be so lonely. One day she said, "I hope you realize that this is not your home. Your father pays to have you stay here!" That was a crusher, to say the least, and so once more I felt like an outsider.

During this time my Aunt Hilda had a little boy named Stewart, whom I came to love very much. He was such a lovely child in every way and his temperament was very sunny. As he grew a little older, we made up all kinds of games together, and his laughter just filled the house.

When he was about four years old he began to feel tired all the time and his little face was always white. I learned one day he was sick and could not play all the games we used to. We saw him deteriorate before our eyes and he was sent to the Great Ormond Street Hospital for Children.

The verdict came back—leukemia.

The full impact did not hit me as it would now, for I was not really aware of the seriousness of the disease until, gradually, I saw his little life sinking rapidly.

He came home from the hospital. They knew it was hopeless, but my aunt and uncle wanted him to be with them as long as he could. He kept calling for me, so I went to stay with him those last days. My last recollection of him was the night before he died when he asked to be able to sit up so he could color a picture. He had such determination, and although he was too weak to even hold the crayon without my aunt's help, he insisted.

The next day he died and Audrey and I found comfort in each other as the funeral arrangements were made. We were taken to see him at the funeral home. It was the first time I had ever seen anyone who was dead. But he looked like a little angel and I could not believe that he would not open his eyes and say, "Come on, Joan, let's play a game!"

Audrey and I attended the funeral—our first. It took place in the lovely old parish church. The little white coffin seemed so very small amid all the splendor. All I knew was that Stewart would no longer be running, jumping, and laughing with us, and I grieved. We were told that he had gone to heaven with the angels. Then he must be with my mother, and that comforted me. She would take care of him.

With Stewart gone, I went back to live with my aunt and uncle.

4

To a twelve-year-old who had already been shunted from place to place, 1939 was a year that held even more changes for me.

My father met me after school one Friday to take me to my grandmother's for the weekend. Just to see my father made me feel so happy and I hugged him before we started the journey. We had not gone very far before he parked the car and told me he had something very important to tell me. I guessed immediately it would be a trip together somewhere.

"No, Joan," he said, "I have some *very* important news to tell you."

I was so excited and tried to guess what it could be.

"Joan, I have met someone and am going to get married again."

I could not believe what I was hearing.

"You see, Joan," he said, struggling to find the words, "I need someone to look after me."

"But I'll look after you, especially when I grow up," I said.

"One day you'll want to marry and you won't want to be bothered with looking after an old man. Your husband will just want to take care of you and your children."

The day arrived when my future stepmother came to my grandmother's house to meet me. She was a very beautiful blonde lady and was elegantly dressed. In fact I had never seen anyone quite like her before. Her black coat had a huge silver-fox collar which framed her face. She was lovely, but I hesitated to welcome her. To me she was competition. Competition for my father's time, and I hoped secretly they would never marry.

Daddy's wedding day dawned, and I awakened knowing that today I would lose him forever. I remembered too that it was also

Saturday and I was performing in a dancing festival. My stomach had butterflies galore as I thought of both events.

As I stood on the stage that afternoon, waiting for the piano to give me my cue, I looked at the clock. 3 P.M. Daddy was getting married at that precise moment. I danced as well as I could, but came in second and won a bronze medal. All the way home I looked at it, but my thoughts were with my father and Ann. I felt very much alone. Death had already taken one parent, now marriage was taking the other.

Looking back now I can see how my father had needed someone. Over the years there have been so many things I have been grateful for. Ann did take care of my father. She gave him another daughter, Geraldine, whose love for me, and mine for her, has grown through the years. Ann gave me a love for literature that I had never known before. She was never without a book and could converse on any subject. Then her love for classical music brought a new dimension into my life which I still cherish today.

I now had to divide my time among three houses. But this was to change drastically. In Europe a man with maniacal ambition brought us into World War II. News filtered over the BBC in London, and I would listen in fright. I wondered how long it would be before Hitler would invade our little country.

It was feared the Luftwaffe's main target for bombing would be London and the suburbs. Hundreds of children were uprooted and sent to the country to escape these dangers. I was evacuated to my paternal grandfather's in Sussex. It was during this time that I first learned what prejudice meant.

I began attending a private school in Burgess Hill, near my grandfather's house. It was very cold and austere, and I had to wear a ghastly brown uniform, complete with brown wool stockings and a shapeless brown hat plonked on my head. I noticed the girls were not at all friendly and only spoke to me if the teacher asked them to. One day a girl approached me and told me she had been sent by the others to ask me a few questions.

"First of all, how long do you intend staying at this school, and secondly, were you evacuated by the Government or privately?"

I told her I had no idea how long I would be attending there and that my father had sent me to stay with my grandfather, which had nothing to do with the Government. The look of relief on her face was incredible.

"We were so afraid you had been evacuated from some poor section of London. This is a very good school, and we wouldn't want the standards to be lowered!"

What a snob! I despised her. I could not believe that anyone could care about things like that, especially in a time of war. That incident made me so angry! I have carried that anger with me whenever I have seen people suffer the sting of prejudice when others have made them feel a lesser human being.

I felt so very lonely in Sussex and finally persuaded my father to let me return. The bombing had not started to any great extent around London, so he thought it would be safe for me to come back. However, it was not long before the incessant attack on that city started, and it became necessary for us to spend a great deal of our time in air-raid shelters. Whenever there was a lull in activity we prepared food to take down with us. To this day I have never been crazy about picnics, perhaps because I had to "picnic" for so long under rather adverse conditions. Nights were spent in the cramped shelter and sleep was not easy, as the antiaircraft guns blazed away and bombs were dropped very close by.

Once school was finished for me at the age of sixteen, I could no longer stand the idea that I was not old enough to do something for my country. I applied for the Observer Corps and was accepted as a "plotter." I had to put down on my application form that I was seventeen and a half, and each payday when I entered the Adjutant's office, I waited for them to find out about me.

My job was to plot the course of friendly and enemy aircraft in the area as I received instructions over my headphones. One night we stood in horror as we began to plot a new weapon that Hitler had unleashed on us—the buzz bomb—a pilotless missile whose warhead brought so much destruction and death to London and the suburbs. As we saw them coming over the radar screen which showed the English Channel, our hearts sank within us. Fortunately, we had such a champion leading our nation. Winston Churchill was an inspiration to all of us, and when listening to his speeches, I felt that I could have suffered anything as long as he was in charge.

The doctor discovered I was beginning to develop an ulcer and advised me to get a medical discharge from the Observer Corps. Reluctantly I had to leave and take up a regimen of fish, milk, and mashed potatoes. I felt such a failure having let Mr. Churchill and my country down!

To add insult to injury, upon arriving home I developed, of all things, German measles!

5

To safeguard against the possibility of a futile attempt at being an actress, my father insisted I take secretarial training. With my mind always on the stage and not on my shorthand, I ended up having ten secretarial jobs in four years. (I never was fired. I always managed to quit before they caught up with my filing system!)

Summer vacations in England were always events to be planned immediately after the Christmas holidays. Working in an office meant asking months ahead for the blessed two weeks I was entitled to. As I changed my jobs so many times, it was a wonder I was entitled to any holiday, but I always managed to work one in somehow. Joy Elson, a friend from school days, would plan her vacation so it would coincide with mine. We could be released from the monotony of the typewriters that shackled us fifty weeks of the year.

One year we went to Bournemouth. We decided to go to the theater one evening—a decision that was to be such an important one in my life. The play was called *But For the Grace of God* and was

written by Frederic Lonsdale. It starred A.E. Matthews, who had
brought such pleasure to the English theater for so many years. He
excelled in comedy and his dry humor delighted his audiences.

We enjoyed the show very much and the next day sat on the
beach discussing it. We looked up and there was A.E. Matthews,
accompanied by some of the cast, walking by us. A little farther
along they sat down. Their laughter kept floating back to us, and I
longed to be able to be part of their company. My life was so
routine—theirs must have such a sense of fulfillment. *Perhaps one
day I, too, will be an actress and travel and not have to be stuck in
an office.*

Joy's voice interrupted my thoughts. "Why don't you go and ask
him for his autograph? I dare you!"

I protested vehemently—saying I had never asked anyone for an
autograph. But she kept on needling me until, finally, I rummaged
in my handbag and found a piece of paper and a pen.

Very hesitantly I walked up to Mr. Matthews and told him how
much we had enjoyed the play and asked for his autograph. He was
very gracious; in fact, he asked us to sit down with them and talk. I
managed to say I had always wanted to be an actress, and he encouraged me to follow my ambition.

The result of the meeting on the beach was that I started dating
the Stage Director. When the play opened in London several weeks
later, I would often go around to meet him and occasionally get to
say hello to Mr. Matthews.

One day it was announced that the show was ending its successful
London run and going on tour again. The Stage Director encouraged me to try out for the understudy to the juvenile lead.

I shall never forget the day I had to go for the audition.

I was working then for the *Courier* magazine near Trafalgar
Square. All day I was so nervous and could hardly concentrate on
my work, knowing that at six o'clock I would be reading for the
understudy part.

At five o'clock when the workday ended, I walked through the
Square, passed Nelson's Column and the magnificent lions, and
found my steps directed to St. Martin's-in-the-Fields—a beautiful

church that I had often gone to on my lunch hour. Now I sat and thought of all this could mean to me. In the quietness of that lovely church I prayed and asked God to help me get the part.

With trembling knees I walked out of the church, almost oblivious of all the activity in the Square, and caught a bus that would take me near the St. James's Theater.

On entering the stage door, I was shown a door which led into the auditorium and told to go down to meet the director, who was sitting in the stalls. I had taken such pains with my appearance. My emerald-green coat, bought especially for the occasion, would offset my blonde hair. My makeup had taken quite a large share of company time. But here I was being ushered through the door which could alter my whole life!

Holding my head high and acting as if I were not in the least nervous, I walked through the door—only to find, too late, there was a step down. As I fell, a raucous *whoops* escaped my lips, reverberating through the auditorium.

That was my grand entrance into the theater!

Two men, who were sitting in the stalls, rushed to pick me up. My hairdo was a shambles. After being told to sit down and regain my composure (which was practically impossible—I felt so humiliated) I met the director.

He asked me what experience I had had and I rattled off as many plays as I could think of, saying I had played in them in repertory, which I knew to be a whopper. Having banged on many agents' doors, and having been told to come back when I had experience, I decided to read as many plays as I could, cast myself in them in my imagination, and dream up a theater where I had been employed.

After talking for a while, the director asked me to read. I walked up the steps leading to the stage and was handed the script and told to read a scene. Afterwards there was a lot of whispering emanating from the darkness of the theater. Finally the director called me to the footlights and said, "Fine! You've got the job of understudy and ASM."

ASM? I hadn't a clue as to what it meant, but I was so excited I shouted, "Thank you," and bounded off the stage, the script tucked under my arm. It couldn't have felt more wonderful it if had been the rarest book in the world. I was told that my salary was to by five pounds (twelve dollars, then) a week. It was less than I made as a secretary, but I didn't care! I was to report for the first reading the following week.

I walked out of the theater ten feet tall! The world was at my feet. Joan Winmill was on her way! On the train home that night, I kept looking at the script in wonderment. I raced up the front door and shouted out to my grandmother, "I'm an actress—I got the job!"

She shook her head incredulously and said she really wasn't sure I was doing the right thing. She had heard many stories of the *goings on* in the theater. One of her warnings to me I remember was, "Don't wear perfume, it makes a man forget himself!" (In my innocence this intrigued me and made me want to wear it to find out what it was he would forget!)

I awakened the next morning with the knowledge that this was the day I would give in my notice at the office. No more Mr. Rumble, whose nose always dripped. He looked like a character out of Dickens, always breathing down my neck and telling me to type faster because of a deadline. As I dressed I kept running back to look at the script, still not really convinced it wasn't all just a dream.

The last day at the office arrived and I said goodbye to the staff. Many had encouraged me in my quest and were delighted for me. me.

The day to attend the first rehearsal dawned and I caught the train to London far earlier than was necessary, for I could not be late. The first reading took place in a rehearsal room in a mews near Baker Street. As the members of the cast and stage crew arrived, my stomach began to churn. They were all strangers to me, except for A.E. Matthews (whom everyone called Matty), because a completely new cast had been engaged.

The director sought me out asking, "Where's the ASM?"

Remembering that is what he had told me I would be, as well as understudy, I hastily made myself known.

"Right," he said. "Here's the working script. Put down the moves."

Moves? I thought, not having any idea what he was talking about.

The last play I had been in was several years ago for the local church and I had not had anything to do with stage management at all.

I was introduced to the stage manager.

"She's your assistant."

Stage manager? I thought. *Then ASM must mean Assistant Stage Manager!*

I hadn't the foggiest notion what I was supposed to do, but decided the best plan of attack was to say as little as possible and listen to everything. ASMs should be seen and not heard. Anyway, that is what this one was going to do.

The cast began to assemble and I was shown where to sit, so I could write down the moves. My common sense told me it had something to do with movements, and as I watched the director instruct the cast, I realized they wanted me to write down his direction. I had managed to work that one out.

I could hardly write fast enough as he called out to the different actors.

"Matty, you cross over up to stage left and stand with your back to the audience, looking into the fireplace."

This went on all day, and when the director asked for the script at the end of the rehearsal, his face was a study.

"You did say you had done this before?"

I nodded, scared to death.

"Have you ever heard of abbreviations? We don't need a running commentary. I can hardly see the script for your scrawl!"

His face looked like thunder, and he shouted for the stage manager.

"Show her the proper way to mark a script and have it done for rehearsal tomorrow."

He turned to look at me once more and started to say something else. Instead, in a fit of exasperation and shaking his head, he swept out of the rehearsal room. To say the least, the stage manager was slightly harassed at the assignment that had been given to him, informing me he had tons of work to do just getting all the props ready. But he tried to explain as patiently as possible to this novice the art of writing down moves.

"The first move should have read—M.X.U.S.L. (Matty crosses up stage left). "This way," he said, "one is capable of still being able to read the script."

We plodded through all my writing, abbreviating as we went until it was all finished.

His tired, "See you tomorrow at nine-thirty," sounded like, *What a dumb blonde I got landed with!*

I went home rather dejected. My first day had not been the most successful or as glamorous as I had expected. Matty had said a few kind words and that had helped considerably. But I realized I had so much to learn.

The next day, "Prompt," was yelled at me. I had been so wrapped up in watching the acting that I had not been following the script. I hurriedly searched through the pages, but by the time I had found the place another actor had given the line that had been forgotten. Another fiery lecture ensued, with a promise from me that I would be more attentive in the future.

As rehearsals proceeded, I found that I knew everyone's lines. This helped if I lost my place in the script, because then there was no hesitation while I looked for the line.

One afternoon as I sat in the prompt corner, I felt a terrific blow on the back of my neck, which sent me flying off my chair. I picked myself up, having seen stars and thinking someone had given me a karate chop. A sandbag had fallen down from the flys, which hold the ropes for the scenery. For days I walked around ungracefully with a very stiff neck! (Years later, after being in a car accident in which I suffered a whiplash, the X-rays showed an old injury to my neck. The doctor asked me if I could remember when this happened. When I answered, "It probably was when a sandbag fell out of the flys," he looked perplexed for a moment, but did not ask any more questions.)

Things were becoming more and more tense at rehearsals. The

girl I was understudying was not working out and they decided to let me have a chance to take over the role. Because I knew the lines and moves (Oh, how I knew the moves!), it was agreed that I could have the part. I was overjoyed, and could not believe that I would actually be in the play—instead of sitting in the prompt corner every night—with all its hazards. I felt very sorry for the other actress. The disappointment to her was tremendous.

The day of departure for Bournemouth arrived. The tour was to open there and an early call was given to meet at the train station. As I packed my trunk I remember thinking, "I'm never going to be unhappy again. At last I am doing what I have always wanted." The secondhand trunk, bought from another actor, was the steamer kind that stood on end. On one side you could hang your clothes, and on the other side there were drawers. Proudly I packed my black makeup case into one of them. Daddy had given it to me years before. Now I would be using it professionally!

The taxi arrived to take me to the station; with a farewell to my grandmother, who stood sadly watching me leave for a life of "goodness knows what," I was on my way to join the rest of the cast.

At the station we all assembled and boarded the train. I saw the new ASM, busy helping load props, and I breathed a sigh of relief. It was too much like hard work and I imagined having to do it every week!

Dress rehearsal was chaos, especially for me. I made my first big entrance looking like a real glamour girl (or so I thought) dressed in a long, black silk skirt and white blouse. My makeup had taken me ages to do, trying to remember all the shading and tricks from school days. There was a scream from the stalls and the director leaped onto the stage, his eyes blazing. His hands smeared my makeup all over my face, mixing the rouge with the mascara.

"Don't you *ever* appear on a stage looking like that again. You look like a circus clown—and those clothes!" He threw up his hands in horror.

He shouted for the dresser to see that I had something else to wear for the performance that night. The leading lady, Joan Seton,

was to help me with my makeup. But I was to carry on through
dress rehearsal with my makeup smeared, "...to teach you to be
professional!"

Mortified was the word to describe me!

Several of the cast who had seen the incident whispered words of
encouragement, and through my tears (some emotional, others in-
duced by the mascara that was rubbed into my eyes) we proceeded
with the play. Here I was playing the bright, happy, juvenile lead—
it took a great deal of acting in that dress rehearsal to keep going.

Afterwards Joan Seton was very kind and helped me buy the
right makeup and apply it. The dresser managed to rustle up a very
pretty white dress, and the minutes ticked away until *Curtain Up*
would be called.

I was so nervous. But so was everybody else and that helped.
Matty said, "If you're not nervous you'll never be any good as an
actress. I'm always scared before I go on, but once I make my first
entrance, everything is all right." He was eighty; I was nineteen; so
I thought, *Then this must be normal—I'll just hope I can get the
lines out.*

The call boy knocked on my dressing room door and called,
"Beginners, please" (for those who open the first scene). I looked
in the mirror and thought, *I'm a real beginner in more ways than
one, but here I go!*

I stood by the door leading onto the set. Looking down I saw a
large electric wire and socket directly in my path. This would hinder
me from running in, so I decided to move it out of the way; an
electric shock swept through me, and I stood completely numb. In
this shocked state I made my first entrance onto the legitimate
stage. I had fallen into the theater for my first audition—now I was
shocked into my first entrance!

The play was received very well, and I stood excitedly in line with
the rest of the cast to receive the applause. It had been worth being
bawled out, and with a wink and a hug from Matty, I felt everything was just perfect.

Afterwards we all stood around and talked about the way the
play had gone. I felt it was confession time. "Thou shalt not lie"

had been drummed into me so much as a child. In front of everyone including the director, I admitted I had never had any professional stage experience before.

"Strange," he said, "I had a feeling you hadn't!" But there was a twinkle in his eye and he seemed to approve of my performance, so all was forgiven.

As I went to sleep that night, my thoughts went back to that chance meeting with Matty on the beach. Perhaps it had not been chance after all. Here I was back with the same play in Bournemouth—the place where it all had begun—and its title was *But For the Grace of God*. I remember praying that He would help me get the job—but I don't remember thanking Him.

We toured for many weeks to Wales, Scotland, Brighton, and other towns. I even got to play at the Wimbledon Theater, where as a child I had seen so many pantomimes.

In each town I would always seek out the oldest church and often sit there in the peace and tranquillity, imagining the many lives that had come and gone and what their effect had been on the community. One of my great interests has always been architecture; there seemed a sense of belonging for me to see the handiwork of artisans who, down through the centuries, had created these oases amid the man-made stresses of life. The stained-glass windows, depicting scenes from Christ's life, would make me reflect on His teachings.

Realizing I was so green to the theater, the cast teased me increasingly, all good-naturedly. Their incredible tales of experiences in the theater left me aghast, never really sure if they were true or not. But I figured I was learning, and maybe one day I would be able to regale people with such tall tales.

Traveling with a touring company introduced me to theatrical boardinghouses. Each town had its recommended ones, and I usually left it up to the experience of others as to where I should stay. I remember one in particular in Wales. It was run by an eccentric, retired singer, who spoke in the manner of the Grand Dame. The house was a dark, overembellished Victorian house, which was advertised as a "home away from home." Everywhere were handwritten notices.

As soon as you entered the toilet, a note warned you, "Do not slam the toilet lid down, it throws my piano out of tune."

There was another sign which read, "Pull Hard and Hold," the toilet being the hanging-chain variety of plumbing—circa 1890.

One morning, after being in there for quite a while and endeavoring to obey the sign (over and over again I tried to get the toilet to flush), I finally emerged for breakfast.

The cast members grinned as I entered the dining room. "Well," said one, "I guess you didn't pull hard enough or hold long enough!"

The landlady, dressed even at breakfast time as for a concert (complete with baubles and beads), stared at me saying, "You're very late for breakfast, young lady. My good cooking gets spoiled waiting, you know."

I often wonder if her large aspidistra plant died after we left, for as soon as she would leave the room, most of her "good cooking" was hidden under its leaves.

The margarine, not butter, was mixed with cornstarch—"very good for you." Her bathtub was filled with vegetables—"helps keep them fresh." When asked if I could take a bath, she reluctantly said, "If you insist—but only use three inches of water and put the 'veg' back afterwards."

Our week was spent hauling vegetables back and forth out of that bathtub; when they appeared cooked on the table and her grace had returned to the kitchen, they were immediately shot into the aspidistra pot.

We managed to fill up on tea, crumpets, and jam in little tea shops in the town and decided to take that particular boarding-house off of our list should we pass that way again.

The tour was coming to a close, and everyone was beginning to wonder where the next job would come from. I had not been able to save anything, even though my salary had been raised to eight pounds (about nineteen dollars) per week, after I had graduated from understudy. My lodgings each week took a great percentage of this, and then the tea shop fill-ups did not help my exchequer. I must say there were days when I longed for my grandmother's cooking.

When the tour ended back in London, I was grateful for the extra money that came in through doing many commercials for fashions, jewelry, breath-fresheners, or whatever I could get. I did so many ads for different shampoos, I was afraid I was becoming typecast.

Matty was going into another play headed for the West End, the Broadway of London. He offered to put in a good word for me to understudy. Naturally, I was delighted to think I might be working with him again, especially in London. He did get me the job of understudying two parts in *The Chiltern Hundreds*. I had met the producers, Linnit and Dunfee, and read for the director.

Each day I sat at the back of the stalls making notes in the script while rehearsals proceeded. I was to understudy the leading juvenile role of the American girl and the lengthy part of the maid. I listened constantly to the accent of Leora Dana, the American actress whom I was to understudy. Going over and over in my mind how she would say each word, I tried to catch every inflection.

The play opened at the Theater Royal, Brighton, where I had appeared before in *But For the Grace of God*. On opening night the tension was terrific. The author, William Douglas Home, paced up and down at the back of the stalls, looking as if he were ready to make a quick exit should the play bomb! The director stood silently watching, almost in shock throughout the performance. But it was received very well, and the audience seemed to get every laugh line. We had a small party afterwards, and again I felt the excitement of being connected with that magical world, the theater.

London's opening night of *The Chiltern Hundreds* in the small, intimate Vaudeville Theater, was the kind of event this girl from the suburbs had never before witnessed—only read about and dreamed of. I could hardly believe I was rubbing shoulders with London's society and celebrities. I was always watching, learning, and rehearsing in my mind how one should behave—react.

The play was a great success. The first-night audience seemed to love it as soon as the curtain went up. Matty was in top form and so were the rest of the cast. William Douglas Home behaved once more like a caged tiger throughout the performance, only to receive well deserved calls for *Author* at the end of the show. There was no doubt this was a winner.

Afterwards the cast was invited to a party hosted by Randolph Churchill, the son of Winston Churchill. Although the under-studies were not included, Diane Hart (who played the part of the maid so delightfully) smuggled me in with the group. Anyone knowing Diane would not be surprised at anything she did! She has been blessed with a gregarious, unpredictable nature that sweeps you along with it. The producers, Linnit and Dunfee, were at the party. Mr. Linnit terrified me. He was always immaculately dressed—usually in a black coat and pin-striped trousers; his dark hair was distinguished by gray sideburns, and he was very dignified and sophisticated. I kept out of his way. Everyone was congratulating the cast on their performance and there was a feeling of great jubilation.

The next morning it was back to rehearsals for the understudies. I was busy being an American girl one moment and a Cockney maid the next.

Only two weeks after opening night I learned that British Actors' Equity was making it impossible for Leora Dana to stay on in the show. She was an American, and the part could be played by an English actress who specialized in American parts. London was full of American shows at that time it seemed. *Oklahoma!* was playing at the Drury Lane Theater and many English actors were out of work.

Leora appealed, as did Linnit and Dunfee, but to no avail. She was given two weeks notice, and then the part had to be taken over by someone else. Being her understudy I got the chance to try out for it; with fear and trembling I faced the fact that I would have to do a scene for Mr. Linnit!

I just had to get that part. Unfortunately, only two days before I had to audition for Mr. Linnit I had fallen down some concrete steps at a football stadium and knocked myself out. As I went through the scene with the producer and director out front, my posture to say the least was extraordinary. I couldn't even raise my head properly and was *so* stiff.

I heard Mr. Linnit say, "She moves so strangely!" The director assured him I was just getting over an accident. It seemed my theatrical career would always have falls in it. It was finally agreed I could have the part.

It was unbelievable! A leading role in London!

Now came a frenzy of fittings for costumes and rehearsals with the cast (many were not happy at all with the change or the fact that they had to have extra rehearsals). I spent every performance out front watching and learning until that final night when Leora played the role for the last time. She was a very sensitive, understanding person, as well as being an excellent actress. Her ability was proven by the Tony award she won on Broadway later in *The Last of Mrs. Lincoln*.

The fateful Monday morning dawned. I was to rehearse the complete play with all the cast and all my new clothes. Some of them just "walked" through their lines, as if their minds were far away, which was very disconcerting to say the least. Matty whispered helpful suggestions and generally encouraged me. Michael Shepley, who played the butler, only just tolerated me, I would say.

Then, all too soon it seemed, I was sitting in my dressing room making up for the performance that night and surrounded with telegrams and flowers wishing me good luck. My face seemed to be burning with excitement, and my stomach had a whole colony of butterflies careening around.

My first appearance came right at the beginning of the play; I was asleep on the sofa with my head covered by a newspaper, attired in a white blouse and red shorts—short shorts. This meant having to make up my legs, and my hands shook as I applied the suntan.

Some of the cast knocked on my door to wish me luck, and then came the knock I dreaded. "Beginners, please!"

I thought back to Bournemouth. It seemed only yesterday that I made my first stage entrance, and now here I was in the West End of London! Happiness was being an actress. I had arrived!

I arranged myself on the sofa, put the newspaper over my face, and just hoped people would not be able to see my knees shaking. The overture seemed to go on forever, and then finally, I heard the curtain going up. Matty made the audience laugh immediately by doing some little bit of business, then the scene started, and I listened for my cue. No words would come out, I was convinced. I heard Matty saying something about the "playing fields of Eton" and I was sitting up saying, "Say, is it really true they won old Waterloo on the campus there?" My mouth had actually opened and *words* were coming out!

When the show finished, the director came around backstage and gave me a hug. Colin Chandler—what a gentle soul he was—I was so lucky to have someone like that as a director.

As I sat in my dressing room taking off my makeup, I heard a knock on my door, and there stood Mr. Linnit.

I'm fired! was my first thought.

He came in and said that he was delighted with my performance and to keep up the good work. Only a few minor revisions were needed. I could not believe it and stuttered and stammered my thanks. Then the author, William Douglas Home, came round and said he approved, too. Afterwards we went out to celebrate at the Savoy Hotel, and I felt as if I were on a mountaintop.

Weeks turned into months as the show successfully went on. Word would come backstage that certain celebrities were out in the audience and we would sneak a look at them through the peephole in the scenery. One night Cary Grant sat in the second row. I found it very difficult to concentrate for that performance!

Then the Queen and Prince Philip, together with Princess Margaret, came to see the play. There was such a feeling of excitement that night! I found it hard to believe that Her Majesty, whom I had watched grow up and had grown to love and respect, was sitting there watching *me*.

Perhaps the most difficult performance was when Queen Mary came to a benefit matinee. The audience consisted mainly of actors and actresses. Knowing Sir Laurence Olivier and others of his caliber were in front did not help my nerves one bit.

No one laughed for what seemed an eternity. We proceeded with the first act trying to be as normal as possible, but wondered desperately what was wrong. Then when Matty came to the line, "I want my bloody sausages!" a laugh was heard from the box facing stage left. Out of the corner of my eye I could see Queen Mary, sitting there so regally, but laughing delightedly. Immediately, everyone in the audience did too. We realized they had all been waiting for her to respond first, a matter of etiquette as it were. After that, the show went very well, and Her Majesty enjoyed it tremendously.

What an imposing royal figure she was. When she died a whole era came to an end. She was greatly loved by her subjects because she genuinely was interested in their welfare. I have since read that she was a dedicated Christian and was known, on occasion, to give religious tracts to visitors.

As to my own life, it seemed I was always out to some party or dinner. Life was very exciting. Meeting people like Sir John Gielgud and the cream of London's theater, plus many from society, kept me in a constant spin. What I did not realize was that my health was beginning to suffer because of my lack of experience both on stage and off—coping with my new life was getting too much for me. I began to muff my lines.

"Can't understand the girl," I heard Marjory Fielding say one night. She played the part of Lady Lister, opposite Matty, and was an elderly, respected actress. She suggested I go to her old voice coach, a lady who lived in Earls Court.

gested I go to her old voice coach, a lady who lived in Earls' Court.

Her apartment was like something out of Charles Dickens's *Great Expectations,* with cobwebs everywhere and a feeling you

were entering the past. She was a tiny, wizened old lady who looked
like an extinct bird. But she knew her job, and it was fascinating to
listen to her. She explained that every consonant and vowel was like
a note of music, and we would go over and over a sentence listening
for each sound. She made it seem as if we were working on some
great oratorio, and her enthusiasm inspired me.

But back at the theater I was getting into trouble with Michael
Shepley, who played the butler. Maybe he resented me because I
was a newcomer. One night he asked me to come to his dressing
room and there proceeded to shout at the top of his lungs about
idiots in the theater. "You repeatedly step on one of my laugh lines
by moving. Get this into your head...when *I* am speaking, don't
even blink an eyelid. Is that clear?" I nodded, stunned by the outburst, and as I left he screamed down the hall, "Let that be a lesson
to you!" and slammed his door full blast.

Everyone had heard the outburst, and I was completely shattered. It seemed I could take any criticism from Matty, because he
would quietly suggest a better way to do something and then en-
courage me to try. But with Michael Shepley—I was now terrified
of our scenes together. I also knew Marjory Fielding was becoming
more critical of my performance. My dresser Chrissy helped me
through many difficult times. She was a warm, dear person, and
many a night I cried on her shoulder as my nerves began to crack.

Then one night the frightening experience of forgetting my lines
occurred, and even though they were being hissed at me from the
prompt corner, I couldn't even remember what scene I was in. Of
course it was a scene with the butler! Then, as he filled in some
lines, it seemed I came back to consciousness and finished, but I
was very shaken. I waited for another dressing down but just got a
look this time. But a look that spoke volumes!

Utterly dejected, I began going to a doctor who told me that, unless I could rest for a month, I was heading for a breakdown.

"Rest? How can I?" I thought. "They would fill my part so
fast—it would mean the end of my playing June." So I struggled
on, but with the help now of some phenobarbital.

William Douglas Home learned I was not well and offered to

send me to his family estate in Scotland for a rest. I shared my fear of not being able to come back in the show, and he assured me everything would be fine and urged me not to worry. Everything was arranged, and I was put on a night train to Scotland—to be met by the butler early next morning. When I arrived at Castle Douglas it was still dark. I had imagined it would look like a typical castle, with a moat; but the family home was a beautiful Scottish mansion, situated in the rugged countryside, with heather on the hills.

Everyone was still asleep, and I was ushered quietly into my bedroom and left to rest. At lunch time there was a knock on my door, and as it opened I got my first glimpse of William's mother, Lady Home. She was a very aristocratic lady with finely etched bone structure and a regal bearing. She asked if I were comfortable and told me to stay in bed as many days as I liked. Then William's sister, Bridget, came in to meet me—she was a delightful person. Over the weeks I grew so fond of the whole family.

As I grew stronger I would sit at the window and look out at the magnificent scenery. That was therapy in itself. On the lawns I could see the rabbits playing unheeded.

When I finally emerged downstairs and met the Earl of Home, I was in complete awe of him. I had never met an Earl before. The characterizations in the play *The Chiltern Hundreds* were based quite largely on William's family (Matty played the Earl). So when I met his father and watched the butler serving meals (much like Michael Shepley), I began to feel as if I were still in the play.

"Welcome, my dear," said the Earl. "Do hope you are enjoying your stay."

I thanked him profusely and said I was feeling so much better already. Just to be able to sit and look at the beautiful scenery and watch the rabbits frisking on the lawn was a pleasure.

"What!" he shouted. "Rabbits! Great Scot! I hire a gamekeeper to keep them down." He rang the bell furiously.

The butler answered and listened to instructions to bring his gun *immediately*. He then proceeded to take potshots out of the windows. If only I had said nothing! I held myself personally responsible for their demise.

The Earl gave me many moments of sheer joy. He was a wonderful man, with a tremendous sense of humor, but his unintended humor caused me to stifle many a laugh.

On one occasion we were all seated around the beautiful Georgian D-end dining table, and the butler had just served the soup. Out of the corner of my eye, I saw the Earl's glasses fall off the end of his nose and into his soup bowl. I could hardly believe it and caught Bridget's eye; she began to laugh too. Lady Home noticed what had happened and said, "Your glasses." "What about my glasses?" asked the Earl. "They are in your soup," said Lady Home. "Great Scot," he said. He promptly picked them up and put them in his pocket without wiping them. Lady Home's face was a study, and it took all the control I could muster not to explode.

In addition to having delightful company to help me to recover, I walked many miles alone over the hills. What a tremendous release it was for me to be able to think unhindered by any noise—except perhaps the occasional sheep dog's bark or the sound of bagpipes being played by the shepherd's little son. Perhaps, in my search for happiness, I had missed enjoying the simple beauty that God had created. But there always seemed to be this driving force within me, urging me on. But to where? I seemed to be on a treadmill and there was no way off. Even amongst such beauty, I longed to return to London and get back to the play.

After two weeks we moved over to the Homes' other Scottish estate, The Hirsel. It was even larger than Castle Douglas, and I spent many hours exploring the house and grounds.

There were many corridors which led to all parts of the immense house. One day I turned the wrong way and opened a door which led to a wing that had been closed off. It had been the children's wing obviously; for there, as if they had only been played with yesterday, the toys of a bygone era still remained. The rocking horse still stood, as if waiting for a rider who imagined himself on some important mission which might save Scotland from the attackers—the English, of course! I sat by one of the windows and thought how quickly they all must have grown up (including William's brother Alec, who became prime minister), and how the whole character of the house must have changed when the nursery wing no longer rang to the laughter and tears of its charges. My childhood had been so different. The rocking horse which I rode on each day stood in my grandmother's kitchen. But it was enjoyed equally as well; a child of six is not aware of the difference in surroundings, but is only aware of what is innate in all of us—the need to be loved.

One day we visited the home of the Duke and Duchess of Buccleuch, Drumlanrig Castle, and had tea with the dowager Duchess. That night they were having a dinner for Princess Margaret, and so the Duchess took us into the dining room to see it set formally for the occasion. The exquisite china and silver that awaited the royal guest glistened amid the magnificent antique furniture.

"If only I belonged in this circle," I thought. "How wonderful it would be to mix with all these people. But I know I don't belong. I don't seem to belong anywhere...."

My stay with the Homes was coming to an end, and I prepared to go back to London. The problems I'd had all seemed like a nightmare to me amid such peaceful surroundings. I dreaded meeting everyone again. I just hoped the symptoms would not return; at least I did not stutter any more, and I had been able to eat normally once again, so my strength had returned.

On arrival at the station the noise of London hit me hard, but it was good to be back again. The stage doorkeeper welcomed me back, and soon it seemed everyone was saying welcome home! I ran down the steps leading to my dressing room with a determined attitude. I would not get ill any more and I would not forget my lines. In fact I would give the best performance I had ever given. It was good to be back and I tried to forget the warnings of the doctor. There was so much to achieve.

Recently Diane Hart, who was with me in *The Chiltern Hundreds,* told me I came back very snooty, talking about tea with the Buccleuchs and my fabulous stay in Scotland. William was taking me to dinner quite regularly and this quite annoyed Diane. However, one night Prince Alexander of Yugoslavia came around to the stage door, asking to see Miss Hart. The stage doorkeeper called

down the stairs, "Prince Alexander of Yugoslavia for Miss Hart!"
Diane ran to the foot of the stairs and whispered to the doorkeeper,
"Say it again—only *louder!*"

He did, and I got the message!

7

During the two-year run of *The Chiltern Hundreds,* I met many
famous people. But the one who, perhaps, had the greatest effect
on my life was introduced to me by the author of the play.

He stood there with his freckled face and white, toothy grin, ra-
diating a dynamic personality, even in those days. Robert F. Kennedy was then studying law at the University of Virginia. Part of
his summers were spent in Europe. This was the start of a deep
friendship which was often filled with arguments on the pros and
cons of England and America.

I remember a visit we made to Chatsworth, the magnificent
home of the Duke of Devonshire. Bobby's sister Kathleen Kennedy had married the Duke's son, Lord Hartington; she and her
husband were later tragically killed in separate plane crashes. Bobby
deeply loved his sister and often made the trip up north to visit her
grave which was located close to the Devonshire estate.

It was at these times, as I traveled with him, that I grew to see the
tremendous loyalty and love that Bobby had for his family. He
would regale me with many stories of life at Hyannisport. His
mother, he said, was very strict, but loved and revered by her family. She would not allow them, for instance, to sing the rather racy
popular song "Everything's Up to Date in Kansas City" from *Oklahoma!* He would grin when telling me this, but you could sense
the great respect he had for her. Her example kept Bobby attending
Mass wherever he was in the world.

I would be teased unmercifully about my Protestant upbringing and would get back at him as often as I could. Once when we were attending Mass at Westminster Roman Catholic Cathedral in London, I noticed a sign attached to the pew in front of me which read, "Beware of Pickpockets!" "Well, old sport," I said, "at least we don't need to warn you about them in Westminster Abbey, our bastion of Protestantism." Then ensued an argument that we had swiped the Abbey from the Catholics in the first place, which was far worse than mere pickpocketing!

On another visit to Chatsworth, we traveled up with Bobby's friend, George Terrien. They tried to teach me to drive as we went through the villages on our way up North. The scared looks on the faces of the villagers, plus the astonished countenance of a policeman on a bicycle, finally convinced them I would need to go to a driving school before I could safely venture forth.

On our arrival at Chatsworth we were shown to our rooms. Mine was way down a long marble hallway; statues lined the walls on either side—some were of the romantic period, others were fierce and forbidding. In the daylight, when I had arrived, it had not concerned me; but when it was time to go down for dinner, I looked out hesitantly. With the coming of twilight the long corridor looked ominously foreboding. In the dim lighting the shadows from the statues were eerie. I decided to walk fast and sang softly "Onward Christian Soldiers" to give me a little courage!

Suddenly, I stopped—listening. I was sure I had heard breathing coming from one of the statues. But it must have been my imagination! On I walked, knees knocking. Then there was a loud scream, and Bobby and George jumped from behind two statues and pounced on me. I let out a blood-curdling yell which emanated throughout the halls and down to the baroque dining room. When we finally entered, there were many pairs of eyes upon us, but none of us ventured any explanation!

Being a lover of history and antiques, I got Bobby to spend many hours with me browsing through the magnificent rooms at Chatsworth. I have always loved anything that has been made by a craftsman's hands, so when I came to the library with its incredible

French tapestries, I could not help but exclaim to Bobby how truly beautiful they were. To think that each stitch had been done by hand!

"Oh," he said, "in America we could turn that out in a factory in no time!" He pretended to be not in the least impressed with any of the incredible treasures that surrounded us. It made me so mad, and that started a big argument about materialism and its pitfalls. But then he started to talk about America and what it stood for; his hopes and dreams were that one day all that the founding fathers had hoped for would come true—that there *would* be equal opportunity for all some day. His philosophy was that you did not deserve happiness unless you gave it.

One of the most treasured gifts he gave me was John Gunther's book, *Inside America,* which I studied avidly.

Bobby's friendship came at a time in my life when I felt as if I had really escaped from my suburban background and now could mingle with London's society. The fact that I was an actress meant I had a "passport" to many places I would never have been asked otherwise.

But there were rumblings coming from Hyannisport that my "passport" did not bear a visa stamped with the approval of the head of the Kennedy family. Bobby told me that one night at dinner his father, Joe Kennedy, had suddenly announced over dessert that he understood Bobby was seeing an actress, an English actress, one who was appearing at the *Vaudeville Theater!* The tone of voice did not hold tidings of joy and Bobby did not pursue the conversation any further.

I had three strikes against me, maybe. One, I was an actress. Two, to make it worse, I was an English species. (When Joe Kennedy was ambassador to England, he was not too popular with its citizens. That is putting it mildly! I had seen evidence of this when Bobby and I would go into a restaurant. Sometimes very pointed remarks were overheard regarding Bobby and his father. On several occasions, Bobby's Irish temper would almost burst, and friends would restrain him from taking a punch at the offending patron.) The third strike against me was that I was appearing at the Vaudeville Theater. The very word *vaudeville* must have made it sound like I was a stripper! Actually, I have never understood why the Vaudeville Theater was so named; its past, which dates back to 1870, holds many famous names and plays. Henry Irving made his first appearance on the London stage there; James Barrie's *Quality Street,* Ibsen's *Hedda Gabler,* and many more outstanding plays were premiered there. But I cannot find anywhere in its history that it was ever used as a variety or vaudeville theater.

Later that summer, I was introduced to Bobby's sister, Jean, and another delightful person, Ethel Skakel. Ethel's enthusiasm bubbled over as she told me how much she had enjoyed the play. She was introduced as a friend of Jean's, which was true. But what I did not realize was that she was falling in love with Bobby. I liked her immediately, for there was a tremendous quality of genuine interest in the other person, and a catching *joie de vivre* that made anyone around her feel caught up in her zest for living. I understand her school yearbook, when she graduated in 1949, aptly described her as, "One moment a picture of utter guilelessness and the next alive with mischief."

Bobby was a very understanding, compassionate person. Beneath his quick wit and seemingly happy-go-lucky personality, was a person who cared about others. He was quick to notice a need. As it was not too long after the war, many things were still scarce in England—especially clothing and luxury items. Bobby would take a mental note of the things I needed and, upon his return to the States, would send "care" packages filled with luxuries I had not seen for years. Soap, perfume, and gourmet foods arrived; I was introduced to Whitman's Sampler chocolates and many other delicacies.

Although I was playing a leading role in *The Chiltern Hundreds,* I was only earning £14 a week. I had taken over the part after the first month and had attained what every understudy dreams of—except a raise in salary. However, trying to dress, live, and tip all the different staff members at the theater each week was a difficult task. I asked the management for a raise. In shocked tones I was told how disappointed they were in me—here they had given me my big chance, and all I cared about was money!

Anyway, Bobby was quick to notice I was having difficulties making ends meet, and parcels arrived with beautiful clothes scrounged from his sisters. (There were labels like Saks Fifth Avenue, Bonwit Teller, and Bergdorf Goodman.) I was overjoyed! At least if my bank balance was not impressive, I looked successful in my beautiful American clothes. Two of the dresses stand out in my mind: a lovely green velvet dress, cut in an Elizabethan style; and a white felt skirt, appliqued with navy, which was topped by a navy silk shirt.

I wore the white-felt-skirt ensemble one evening when my agent took me to a party honoring Errol Flynn. He arrived looking as if he had just debarked from a yacht, dressed in a navy blazer, cravat, and white pants. He was immediately surrounded by a bevy of beautiful girls, and I was sure I had seen the whole scene in one of his movies.

I remember sitting on a settee that night talking to an actor—suddenly someone upset an ashtray all over my white felt skirt. I was mortified. My evening was ruined, when—lo and behold—Cesar Romero emerged from out of the crowd, whisked out his pocket handkerchief and dusted off the offending ashes. It was worth the moment's distress to receive such gallantry from Mr. Romero!

One night, after entering the stage door for almost two years, I saw the final notice on the bulletin board. We were closing in two weeks. The play and the people had become a way of life for me and I dreaded the final night. Many actors and actresses have a dread in the back of their minds that they will never work again. But my dread obsessed me, and on the last night when the final curtain came down, I went back to my apartment utterly dejected. My confidence was sinking rapidly, together with my bank balance.

The play was going to Broadway as *Yes, M'Lord,* and most of the cast were going with it. However, because I was playing an American part, American Equity ruled an American would have to play it. This was fair enough—especially after English Equity had insisted a Britisher play the part in London. I hoped Leora Dana could play the part again. However, this thought did not help the cold fact—most of the cast were going to America, but not me. Apart from the idea of not being with the play, I had always wanted to visit America. Broadway seemed such a glamorous place.

The few of us who were left in London from *The Chiltern Hundreds* would meet in a little restaurant off Piccadilly Circus. It was a meeting place for actors and actresses of all strata and was a fantastic hive of information concerning who was casting what.

To go there I would take as many pains as if I were going to Ascot, for you never knew just whom you might meet. The actors' entrances were incredible and everyone tried to outdo the other. But it was a place to go and not feel like an outsider.

Because I was so nervous I smoked and, to add to the dramatic effect, would use a long cigarette-holder. I really did not enjoy smoking; but it gave me something to do with my hands and added, especially with the holder, a sense of sophistication which I really did not have.

News of auditions would filter through over tea, and I would make mental notes to call the casting offices. Agents who had been interested in me during the run of *The Chiltern Hundreds* were called, and each day I waited, hoping.

William Douglas Home knew I was having difficult times financially, so he asked me to do some secretarial work for him. (My father was right! He wanted me to have something to fall back on when he insisted on my secretarial training!)

One day while sorting William's mail, I came across a letter which was opened and waiting to be filed. It was from Matty and he told of the reception they were having in America. It sounded so exciting playing on Broadway—I longed to be there. Then a sentence hit my eye and crushed me deeply. "At last we have a real June—Elaine Stritch is great in the part!" Matty—who had been my mentor, my idol, was saying, "At last we have a *real* June!" He had told me so often how good I was, how pleased he was. Now my confidence, not only in myself but in other people, hit zero.

I put the letter down and walked out into the street and made my way to St. James's Park to recover. I fed the ducks and the swans automatically, for I was deep in thought remembering all the wonderful things Matty had said about my performance. Were they true or not? Could I act—or was I fooling myself?

I didn't want to face anyone and I walked to a telephone booth and made a call cancelling an appointment for that evening. I wanted to run, but where? I felt locked inside my body and desperately wanted to free myself of all everyday responsibilities. I went back to my apartment. Closing the door, I felt an utter failure. I didn't want my family or friends to know this, so again the mask had to be readjusted and the "happy talk" well rehearsed so it would not sound too brittle to the hearer.

The one thing I looked forward to were my letters from Bobby, which came regularly, telling of his studies at the University of Virginia, his many escapades, and his hopes to get back to London as soon as he could. I was dating several men, knowing Bobby was dating in America. But to me he was very special and I believe, for the first time in my life, I considered myself to be "in love." Looking back now I believe I was in love with his mode of life. The excitement, the glamour, and needless to say, his financial status. To a girl from the suburbs he epitomized everything one could dream of.

So again I was not prepared for the contents of a letter I received from him a few weeks later. The familiar Hyannisport postmark meant he was home for the summer and would also mean he would probably be heading for London soon.

I opened it, excited at the thought. Then I read, "I am getting married to Ethel Skakel...." I couldn't believe my eyes. She was the girl I had met with his sister Jean in my dressing room that night. It seemed that all my bad news lately came in letters from America.

I did not know then that God knew the future—He was working it out—and that one day in America I would meet His choice for me. Elizabeth Barrett Browning says it so eloquently, "God's gifts put men's best dreams to shame."

Bobby was marrying God's gift to him, and as history testifies, He made no mistake. Ethel was the perfect wife for Bobby. She has a depth that belies the bubbling personality and a resiliency that brought her through the untold agony of seeing her husband assassinated.

Bobby's assassination hit me deeply and brought back many memories of the carefree boy I knew—one who loved life and was anxious to be a contributing force for helping others. His Irish temper could flare, there was a great obstinacy in his nature, but all these traits were used as he fought to help people who had no one to speak for them.

After the news of Bobby's impending marriage, there was only one thing I could do to escape the feeling of utter disappointment—work. I decided not to wait for the two good breaks my agent had told me were in the offing and accepted straight off a contract to appear as a guest star in repertory companies playing the role of June in *The Chiltern Hundreds*.

One engagement stands out in my mind—Aberystwyth, Wales. Upon arriving there, I was told we were to do one-night-stands in the surrounding villages, many of which were way up in the mountains. Very different from what I had imagined! Props and cast were loaded onto a double-decker bus each night, and we set off over winding, bumpy roads to the villages of Wales. It was a far cry from the West End of London!

It was bitterly cold, and we plowed through deep snow to get to some villages. It was the lambing season, and I remember wondering why it was that God had so arranged it that a baby lamb had to endure the hazards of the bitter snowstorms. It seemed they had enough to do just to survive. But they did survive, and it was another miracle that goes on unheeded by so many of us.

One little town I will always remember, even though I have long forgotten its name. We arrived at the "theater"—actually a village hall—ready to perform, only to find the boiler had burst and there was no heat. It was freezing and I had my first entrance in shorts! It was no good throwing any kind of leading-lady tantrums, no one would have cared, and nothing could be done about it. That was bad enough, but some stray cats had made their home in the auditorium. Oh, how that place smelled! In addition to freezing, I thought I would gag to death!

My first scene was a battle between laughter and tears as I remembered my West End days. I looked at the scenery. It was permanent, so one had to improvise one's exits and entrances accordingly. The furniture looked like Salvation Army rejects, and the sight of the beat-up settee that I had to lie on turned my tears into laughter. It was so incongruous to imagine that this was supposed to represent the home of an Earl!

The next week we came back and played *The Winslow Boy* by Terence Rattigan in the same set, with the same furnishings. The boiler had been mended, but the other problem—the cats—had not been remedied! (Where, oh, where was the glamour of the theater?)

Looking back, I would not have missed the experience of the hardships of a one-night-stand touring group. At the time, I felt completely bewildered at finding myself so far from the West End of London and the prestige that went with it. Even then, I can see God had His hand on my life. I had stumbled, literally, into show business without any real on-the-job training or experience. It was good for me, too, to see how others who were so dedicated to their profession put up with hardships. I am glad now that it was not handed to me carte blanche.

Pride raises its ugly head in many forms; when it does in my life, God has very kindly put His loving foot in my path and allowed me to take a fall. I guess He will have to keep on doing it with me, for just when I think I have learned humility and all its attributes—down I go again.

After my stint with guest appearances was over, I returned to London and continued dating an actor I had met. If ever two people were more unsuited to each other we were. But God had a plan, even in this. We saw each other regularly, but there were many tirades. Each of us was trying to find the answers to all our frustrations and longings in each other. There was the constant fear, too, of loneliness. Deep down inside I was afraid of the future, afraid of being alone, even though I had many friends; John basically had the same fears. Perhaps our greatest fear was of being failures in life. I believe so many people are drawn together in this way and that is why there are so many unhappy relationships. For it is not based on real, giving love, but purely on a need to *be* loved.

We worked together on tours and in repertory, and our conflict of personalities made it *Heartbreak House* all the way. I would go off on tour, or he would; everything would be fine until we both hit London, and it would all start again. There was a feeling of futility to our relationship, but there seemed no answer. Whichever way a decision would be made, there had to be the inevitable tearing apart of that which was deep within me.

I kept busy with commercials, TV appearances, and movies, but once more I seemed to be fighting a losing battle with my health. When I was playing Brighton again—this time in George Bernard Shaw's *Arms and the Man* in the role of Raina—I was nearing collapse. I was so exhausted and had lost so much weight it was a struggle just to get to the theater at night. I loved the part, playing opposite Andrew Crawford, and so I struggled on somehow each night.

My friends could see I was not well and suggested I stay on in Brighton in a nursing home for a while. The tour was over after this date, and unwillingly I agreed to this. The thought of a nursing home scared me (all I wanted to do was to get home to London and rest), but I knew I could not look after myself properly. I stayed there for a while, then discharged myself and went home.

After I arrived back in London, it seemed I slept for days. I felt extremely weak; just the thought of even trying to get back to work seemed like an impossible situation. My London doctor again told me to really take care of myself—rest, pay particular attention to my meals, and pace myself—instead of always being active and trying to pursue my career. It seemed as if I were in a complete vicious circle; if I didn't work, I didn't eat; if I did work, I collapsed. There had to be an answer, and I had to find it. I looked at others who seemingly had so much physical strength and I envied them.

After a while I began to find I didn't really care what work I got. Friends would say, "Hold out for the big breaks, don't do any 'B' movies." But my confidence was slowly sinking, and I knew that when I went for interviews I did not make a good impression.

I don't remember how I ever got to audition for *Dracula,* but I do know that once I signed the contract, my fears told me I had done the wrong thing.

As a child I had once seen a filmed coming-attraction for *Dracula.* (I was attending a bland comedy with my grandmother.) I went under the seat until assured that it was over. When we left the performance, we found a booth set up in the lobby with a sign which said, "Dare to Open These Curtains!" Someone did—just as I walked by—and there, life-size, was a model of Dracula staring at me. All the way home I *knew* he was following me. Nanny had to stay in my room that night until I finally fell asleep, having been convinced he was not under my bed. Now I was signed to go on tour with none other than Bela Lugosi, who had created the role in the movie!

I was very hesitant to attend the first rehearsal and meet Mr. Lugosi. He arrived late, making a grand entrance, and was introduced to each of the cast. When it came my turn, I stood there in sheer amazement. He looked just like the wax figure that had scared me so as a child. But he was gracious and very professional as we proceeded with the first reading.

When it came time for the scene in which he was supposed to hypnotize me, I thought, "Here we go! I must not look as if I'm scared of him. After all, this is ridiculous—it is only a play and he really is just an actor." But when he started to look into my eyes, I sensed a strange, burning sensation, and tears began to well up. He stopped suddenly and said, "Child, never look in my eyes. Always look here," and he tapped his forehead. I did just that every time we played the scene after that, and things went along smoothly.

He took playing the part of Count Dracula very seriously, and we were never allowed to change a word, a look, or a move. It was as sacred as Shakespeare to him. Once I heard him say that, perhaps, the worst thing for his career had been the success of *Dracula,* for people would never take him seriously as an actor any more. Apparently he had known great adulation in his homeland of Hungary.

In the final scene, set in a crypt, he was supposed to be in a coffin; the doctor and his friend, Van Helsing, drive a stake in Dracula's heart—the only way he can be killed. But Bela would never get in the coffin and would always give the death scream from the wings. He had a great superstition about this.

The only time we saw him during the day would be when we would meet at the train to move from one city to another. Then he would stride down the platform with his wife and son and disappear into a private compartment, to ride with the shades drawn for the entire journey.

The trouble with the cast was that, after we got over the awe of being with *the* Dracula, our emotions swung the other way. The overly dramatic dialogue became too much for us, and we all started to get the giggles. I cannot begin to describe the agonies we went through every night trying to control our feelings and playing our lines "straight." Once the stage director called us all on stage after a particularly giggly show and said he would fire all of us if we did not stop this appalling laughter. Even as he said this, someone giggled and started all of us off again. We were appearing in a theater way up north of London, and the poor director had no choice but to put up with us. It even got to him finally, as night after night he had to oversee the fake bats and smoke that always preceded Dracula's appearance.

One night the smoke got to me, too. I came to the scene where Dracula was supposed to hypnotize me (just after I gasped in horror at seeing him). The smoke, pumped under his cape each time he made an entrance—with arms wide apart, got down my throat and knocked me out cold. The audience was unaware of what had happened, and somehow Bela ad-libbed his way through the scene—

with me prostrate on the ground. As soon as the curtain came down, I was whisked off to the waiting arms of a St. John's Ambulance man. These men are volunteers who wait around for strange occurrences such as mine, so they can administer first aid. Bela proceeded to direct all the traffic that had gathered. He even prevented brandy being administered to me from a well-meaning member of the cast. "Noooothing by way of mouth," he kept repeating. "Nooooooothing!"

I recovered enough to go on again the next day, but I was very careful not to exclaim too heartily upon seeing Dracula coming through my window.

We returned to London and played all the surrounding theaters, and then our tour was over. I was rather relieved, I must say. Touring had never been my favorite part of theater life, and now perhaps there would be a good break waiting for me.

As it turned out, I landed the leading part opposite Guy Middleton in the movie, *The Harassed Hero*. Then there were more movies, and life seemed to be going along smoothly. Until then it seemed my health had improved, but suddenly I began to see the telltale signs that all was not well. My speech started to slur again, the headaches were becoming unbearable, and the feeling of wanting to run away from it all dominated me.

I was so tired of always acting offstage—trying to be vivacious when I felt completely exhausted. I never seemed able to be myself any more. Perhaps I had always acted! Had I built a façade around myself to protect me from people really knowing me? The mask was being worn more often now, because the last thing I wanted was for people to know the desperation I was feeling.

Where was the happiness I thought I would always have, now that I was an actress?

I thought of all my friends who envied me, and in front of whom I had always acted. I couldn't let them know that, even though I loved the work, there was still something that was unreachable, unattainable. I wanted to find the ultimate in life; but where was it leading me?

I remember, with an almost cold detachment, the advent of my breakdown. It is as if I can see a scene being played out by someone else, but when I look closely the central figure is me—and I do not like what I am watching. It is a scene I would like to erase completely from my life, for the nightmarish memory of it sometimes sweeps over me. If I did not now have the deep assurance of God's love and forgiveness, it would drag me down again into a pit of despair and self-pity.

For weeks I had sensed a feeling of desperation and a longing for peace. It seemed as if the struggle to try to make a career was futile, for my health would so often keep me from attending auditions. When I did, my appearance and reading of the part did not send the producers into ecstasies. My confidence was gone. I dreaded getting out of bed in the morning and having to face people. The thought of even crossing a street would send fear running through me.

What was happening to me? In the past, I had always been game to try anything. I had enjoyed the unexpected telephone call that sent me racing out of the apartment, bound for some delightful discovery. Now, I dreaded to hear the telephone ring. If it were my family, I would have to make up some excuse as to why I hadn't called or been to see them. If it were my agent, I feared he would say he had someone he wanted me to meet, or he had some great part that he wanted me to read for. My friends were the easiest to act with, pretending to laugh at their jokes, saying I was terribly sorry not to be able to make the party but....

I looked at myself in the mirror and saw a person who looked old beyond her years. No amount of makeup could hide the lost expression in my eyes. Someone has said that the eyes are the "windows of your soul." These "windows" were misted over with the effect of so many drugs—prescribed of course, but nevertheless eating away any spontaneity that might still be left. They were red-rimmed from crying. I despised my weakness and, in so doing, despised everything about myself.

Every day I would read in the paper of people who were far worse off than I—people starving, people bereaved. Many times I had wanted to be able to reach out and perhaps help, but always this *me* seemed to get in the way. My life seemed so utterly useless.

One night I was having dinner with a friend. He was proceeding to lay down the law about my career. "You aren't pushing yourself enough! You don't attend enough auditions!" All of a sudden it seemed every fibre of my being was screaming out silently within me, *Peace! That's all I want! I have to get out of here!*

I struggled to the door of the restaurant and left him sitting at the table, watching in amazement. Stumbling into the street, I realized I was losing control of my legs. My mind was reeling, but I knew there was a bus nearby which would take me to my grandmother's house.

With all the willpower I could muster, I stood in line waiting for that bus. When it came I stumbled on and sat down, not daring to look at the other passengers. My hands were wet with an icy sweat, and I dug my nails into the palms, fighting for control. Every nerve seemed to be on edge; a vise seemed to be tightening around my head. The noise from the engine of the bus made my pain excruciating. Every noise jarred me and I fought for control. Oh, just to be able to get to my grandmother's house! Perhaps I could rest there and no one would know. I could keep up the act.

Then the floodgates burst forth and I cried openly in front of all the other passengers. All my desperation poured out—uncontrollably. I could no longer hide behind the mask—always trying to act the perfect lady—always in control. Now I felt naked as they stared.

"How disgusting, she's drunk!" I heard someone say.

I tried to defend myself, but all I could utter were unintelligible sounds. I had no control over my mouth and what came out was a deep cry for help, an agonizing moan.

I had heard these sounds before, years before, when my grandmother had tried to tell me she was ill. Being a child I had laughed, thinking she was playing a game, and had run off to school, not knowing she was asking for help.

My legs felt as if they were trapped in a quagmire, but when the bus reached my stop, I dragged myself past the accusing eyes. I was a gibbering, uncontrollable, frightened human being. My grandmother's house was within a few steps, and I fell in the front door and let out a cry for help.

The next thing I remember was the family doctor standing by my bed saying, "The next time she has one of these hysterical outbursts, call me and I'll give her a sedative immediately."

The next time!

All the floodgates having burst, there was a strange sense of relief; now I would no longer feel this terrible, stifling, meaningless battle within me.

But the doctor had said, "The next time...."

I closed my eyes and cried silent tears, for there seemed no use in trying to battle anymore.

Why was I weak when others could seemingly face life's problems? I longed to be a "cabbage."

That's what I had called people who went about their everyday jobs, content to live a mundane life—catching the same train every day, doing routinely the same job, and returning to the same house to eat, sleep, and start the whole monotonous, dreary round again.

I did not realize that they too were wearing masks—masks to cover their weariness which came from facing the responsibilities that loomed before them day after day.

Perhaps they envied those of us in the creative world, whose lives seemed so full of highs, but who managed, usually successfully, to hide the devastating lows.

I tried to talk but found no words came out, only sounds.

Raising my arms I tried to gesture, but my hands were contorted and would not obey me.

Dear God, what is happening? I can no longer control my body!
I tried to sit up and walk, but could only crawl like an animal.
My feet gave way under me each time I tried to stand.

I began to shake in abject fear as I realized I could no longer rely
on my body to act at my every command. It was as if the home I
had known for so long had been taken over by an outsider who ran
rampant through the hallways of my being. This outsider was
flaunting everything *I* had tried for years to hide—to hide from
spectators who gather to mock and shake their heads.

There are so many incidents I cannot remember regarding my
breakdown because I was under heavy sedation. Sometimes I can
remember vividly something that happened—as if I had only been
caught in a terrible nightmare. But unfortunately, it really happened. One day I remember the doctor said, "You will never be the
same again, Joan. Your whole nervous system has been through a
tremendous strain. You will always have to pace yourself; never let
yourself become overtired, or you will find all the symptoms returning."

I turned my head away, not wanting to hear that I would never
be the same again. I wanted to *be:* to radiate vitality, to be carefree
and strong, to achieve everything that was still waiting out there to
achieve, and to love and be loved. But who would want to have a
burden like me in their life?

I lay there for weeks it seemed, thinking of what my friends had
accomplished. There was Joy Elson, with whom I had been so close
at school and with whom I had spent so many vacations. She had
dared me to get A.E. Matthews's autograph, and that had led to
my becoming an actress. Now she and David Rayner were happily
married and had children; I felt she had achieved so much more
than I. Others I knew were married, happily, it seemed. Had I put
too much of an emphasis on attaining fame at the expense of finding real happiness in marriage and children? One thing was certain
now—I would never have children, for I could not be trusted to be
a mother.

Pace myself. Do not get overtired. It would be laughable to say
to a child, "Sorry, I'm too tired to be a mother today. Come back

when I've paced myself and refueled."

Anyway, I didn't really want children. The thought of my mother's death in childbirth terrified me. Perhaps I would inherit her tendencies and die of toxemia.

Forget the mother bit. Forget the wife bit, too. No man would want this gibbering idiot for a wife.

So what was the point of living?

Would I need to be pepped up with pep pills and to sleep with sleeping pills for the rest of my life? To have to live in this never-never land of drugs and to need to pace oneself was not worth the effort.

Depression followed depression.

I dreaded a new day for it held no bright hope; and I dreaded the nights for they held, even with sleeping pills, either sleeplessness or terrifying nightmares.

My one dread was that everyone was talking about putting me in an asylum. Shock treatment. Locked into a room. Straight-jackets. All these visions would mock me at night, and I would always sleep with the light on for fear I would be suddenly overtaken in the darkness.

My mind was playing tricks on me. It was all I could do to perform the simplest task.

Looking back, it seemed as if I were forever climbing a dark mental staircase, the walls of which were gradually pressing in on me. There seemed no end to the murky, oppressive journey.

It was kept as quiet as possible that I was having "trouble." Oh, how I thank the Lord that terrible stigma is being lifted from those who suffer the indescribable torments of the mind. It is being recognized as a real illness now and not as some imaginary condition one wishes upon oneself.

Society has advanced tremendously since the eighteenth and nineteenth century when it was considered fashionable to stroll past the cages of those who were demented, as one would now stroll through a zoo. But the animals in the zoo today are treated in a far superior fashion to the luckless, defenseless creatures who were then chained and mocked. Medical science is learning more and more about the chemical imbalances that play such an important part in the working of the brain.

The guilt that pervaded me was unbelievable. I had let my family down—no would would ever forget that Joan Winmill had had a nervous breakdown.

I remember that some time later I had fallen, fracturing my right hand. Wherever I went with my hand in the cast, I was shown sympathy. "Yes, it hurts," I thought, "but if you only knew—it's *nothing* compared to the agonies I've been through. This shows; but the pain of hidden agonies is multiplied ten thousand times, because there seems to be no end and no one who can really understand."

My care was becoming too much for my grandmother, and so I moved to my Aunt Hilda's house nearby. Their house had seen so much sorrow, first my mother's death, and then the loss of their little son, Stewart. Now I was to burden them. It was a tremendous task for them, but I was grateful to be there, if only for a while. Audrey was there, and her bright, sunny countenance always seemed to help me.

I lay awake in the bedroom of their house, remembering that this was the same room where my mother had died. What had been her thoughts as she had struggled to live? Did she ask God to help her? If she had lived, would I be locked within the depths of my own prison? Or, would her love and encouragement have filled the void and released this timorous being?

I thought back to my religious training and tried to pray. My words were faltering, so I stopped. The only prayers I had heard were in church, and they had always been so eloquent. But I did remember certain passages of Scripture and those would console me. A few years after my breakdown I found a diary written during that time. There, as a reminder to me of the dark days, were some of the verses from the Psalms that had comforted me. I don't remember the exact verses, but they all had to do with David crying out to God and God hearing him.

One night I had a vivid dream of the Crucifixion. It was as if I were there and actually seeing the soldiers driving the nails into

Jesus' hands. I wanted to cry out to stop them, but I hung back in the crowd, afraid—not wanting to be known as one of His followers.

When they had finished nailing Him to the crude execution tree, the thud of the cross being driven in the ground was horrifying. When I took my hands from my eyes, I looked up and saw that, instead of Jesus on that cross, it was me! I could not help myself, but struggled in the crowd to get to the cross and plead with the soldiers to get me down. I awakened in a pool of sweat and reached for another sleeping pill to drown out the terrifying memory.

I was so tired of not being able to swallow properly and not being able to walk or talk. If I stayed in bed much longer I would be so weak, what would happen to me? I struggled each day to try to talk. One day my cousin Audrey was having a one-sided conversation with me while sitting at my bedside quietly embroidering. Suddenly, I found I could speak again! To hear the sound of my own voice normally uttering *words* was unbelievable! We laughed together, and I felt so thankful that once more I had control of my tongue. (Oh, that I had such control of my tongue in the years to follow!)

What a relief it must have been for them all, as they saw me get stronger each day. I shall always be grateful for the care they gave me, even though it was so hard on them.

Months later, I felt strong enough to return to London, and after a few shaky starts, I was able to work again. But there was always the fear in the back of my mind that someone would bring up the fact that I had had a breakdown and was not to be trusted in any important role.

I had now signed with Plunket Greene, the agent, and he sent me out on many auditions. I landed a part in *The Housemaster*. It was a revival of a classic about a boys' school and the escapades of a professor and his exuberant family. I was delighted with the idea of appearing in the West End of London once more, for we were opening at the St. Martin's Lane Theater. Opening night came, and with it came all the anticipation, nerves, and exhilaration that always accompanies it. *The Housemaster* was very dated, but we played it for all it was worth, and the audience delighted in the rather "campy" way it was presented.

After the curtain came down, we had taken our final bow, and all the effusive accolades had been distributed, I returned to the dressing room deep in thought. "All right. What's missing? I'm back on the West End stage and this is unbelievable. Something is still missing!" My father came round to see me and was so happy that I had made it back in one piece again. So was my stepmother, Ann. Together they wished me happiness and good health from now on.

A red apple on my dressing-room table was a token from John. He had read that is what the Barrymores sent each other on opening night. He was away on tour and could not be with me.

After the show, the cast celebrated, and finally it was time to go home.

I pulled out the key to my apartment and opened it with the thought, "Why am I not on top of the world? This is absolutely ridiculous. I'm back. I'm well again. I love this work. How I love it. The cast had been great. The reception was wonderful. Why? Why? Why? There is a dimension still missing! It seems I am reaching for something that is unattainable—to be satisfied within oneself—to be content—to feel I belong." I automatically reached for a sleeping pill, for I knew it would blot out all of the questions and bring the blessed oblivion once more.

I wondered if being a success was worth the struggle. Always nagging inside me was the realization that I *loved* this work, even with all of its heartaches. For me there would always be a desire to immerse myself in a role and be the character that the author and director had labored over. So it was with a great feeling of bewilderment that I began to see that my work was not enough to satisfy all that was crying out, like a starving lioness, within me.

I went into a serialized, TV thriller, "Epitaph for a Spy," by Eric Ambler, playing the leading role opposite Peter Cushing. Peter is known as the star of so many horror movies, but the roles are completely opposite to his nature. He was a very gracious man, and he and his wife were so helpful to me in so many ways. Perhaps they were unaware of just how kind they were at a time when I desperately needed a helping hand.

With the series came a great deal of publicity in which every actress delights. It was exciting to reach for the morning paper and see your photograph and a good story about you in black and white. Also, with this engagement in "Epitaph for a Spy" I returned to all the parties and social events. It was an exciting time, mixing again with the theater and movie greats, seeing Sir Noel Coward surrounded by his admirers, partying with Sam Spiegel, Bob Hope, and Zsa Zsa Gabor.

As I would look at them the thought would come, "Are you really happy, or is there something deep, deep, down that is missing in your life, too?" Everyone seemed so sure of themselves, so confident. Perhaps it was only I who expected more out of life.

I found I was now analyzing every word I said and others said to me. I would wake up in the morning remembering my conversation at a party or over dinner. Had I said the right thing? What did they mean when they had said so and so? The mask was being fitted more securely this time. I was determined that no one should ever find out that I needed anything or anybody to make me completely happy. I had not come to realize like Saint Augustine that our soul can never find rest, until it finds its rest in God.

One day, during a rehearsal for a further segment of "Epitaph for a Spy," I knew my health was cracking again. The guilt that pervaded me whispered over and over again, "You're letting your family down, you've got to keep going. Your love affair has to end. It's a dead end for both of you. You have to be free—free of all your mistakes."

There seemed no way out of the maze that trapped me, for I did not have the strength to make a definite decision about anything. I could not face another breakdown with all of its heartaches and suffering—not only for myself, but for those I loved!

The thought of suicide began to dominate my mind. It is so strange to many that, though I had a good general knowledge of the Bible, the act of suicide did not seem to me a sin. The dictionary defines suicide as "self-murder." I had never thought of it in that way—especially then. For here was a life that was not bringing happiness to me and certainly not to others.

I had once thought seriously of doing some kind of welfare work—particularly among prisoners. I would often think as I read the reports of trials in the newspapers, "There but for the grace of God go I." I realized the need for punishment to deter crime, but imagined what it would be like to be imprisoned—to hear the door of that cell clang shut and to have to face the self-recrimination for seemingly endless days, perhaps for a crime committed on the spur of the moment!

I was a virtual prisoner—in my mind. So how could I help others? Imagination ran rampant, spurred on by the phenobarbital. Depressions brought me down to the pit of despair.

Sorry for myself? Yes.

Longing for an answer? Yes, oh, yes.

But where?

I walked for hours in nearby Kensington Gardens. The bleakness of winter still pervaded the park, but for a while I was free to get things in perspective as I felt the soft grass underfoot. The gray sky overhead helped me to vent my feelings of wanting to be free.

In the streets of my beloved London there seemed to be endless souls all bent on finding their own solution to the pursuit of happiness. In William Blake's poem, "London," he wrote:

> I wander thro' each charter'd street,
> Near where the charter'd Thames does flow
> And mark in every face I meet
> Marks of weakness, marks of woe.

Did we all have an imaginary Shangri-la that we escaped to, only to find in the morning's harsh light that it had faded, and the stark reality of one's existence loomed only too frighteningly?

In all these depths of thought, the images of my father's face and my family would come before me. If I killed myself, what grief it would bring to them—particularly to him. He had always been so kind, always wanting to help. I remembered the long talks we would have, sometimes parked in his car before he left for a trip, or when he came to meet me after he returned. These memories would check me and in my confusion brought an island of refuge.

But the secure feelings faded as the torment grew stronger and stronger, until finally I became obsessed with the thought of ending my life. It was then, in all my despair and confusion, I cried out to God to help me.

I can *never* believe in the *God is Dead* idea; the events that took place so quickly in my life, after I finally reached the place of knowing I needed Him, bear testimony that He is very much alive and is concerned for all our earthly and spiritual needs.

So it was that, at this dead-end phase of my life, with seemingly no answer to my most fervent needs, the most important telephone call came. The phone rang and rang in my apartment until I finally answered it.

The caller inviting me to hear Billy Graham was not even aware that God was using him to start me on life's most important and fulfilling venture.

It was an eternal journey—one that had a beginning, but no end—and one where I would be *no longer alone*.

I had carefully selected what I would wear to the Billy Graham Crusade meeting. No one was going to think by my outward appearance that I had a need. This was Miss Successful who had really only come to be an observer and to enjoy the company of some friends. The bright red coat with the brass buttons belied what it was covering. Here was a person so desperately unhappy that she cried herself to sleep most nights while she waited for the sleeping pills to blot out the anguish.

The phenobarbital would give me courage to meet John Mercer and his wife who had invited me to the Crusade. I was in a vicious circle; my nerves were cracking, and taking the barbiturate to keep me going filled me with a hopeless depression.

But tonight I would act as if nothing was wrong with my world. Taking a quick look in the mirror, I decided I looked successful, and when I smiled, everyone would think my life held no problems. In four words—I was a fake.

After dinner with several friends of the Mercers, we headed towards Harringay Arena where the Crusade was being held. One person remarked that he couldn't wait to see the crying converts. There had been an article in one of the London newspapers about this, and we laughed and agreed it would be interesting. Even as I laughed I sensed a terrible need in my life, but these people would never know, I assured myself.

After we were seated in the Arena, I began to look around at the people. It was incredible! It seemed like a vast cathedral. The large choir was singing "Blessed Assurance, Jesus Is Mine." It was an unfamiliar hymn to me, and the words seemed almost foreign. *Blessed Assurance?* I felt none. *Jesus Is Mine?* Not really. He died for the sins of the *world*. He could never be said to be mine.

I looked at the people who sat on the platform. One lady stood out; she was wearing a bright-red coat and an exotic yellow hat. I thought it must be Sophie Tucker. Never had I seen anyone dressed in such bright colors attending a religious service! Weeks later I was to meet that person, Miss Henrietta Mears from the Hollywood Presbyterian Church, whose life had been used to bring so many to Christ. She was to influence my life, too.

A surprise for me at the Crusade was the appearance of Dale Evans Rogers who told of her love for Jesus Christ and how He had changed her life. It was amazing to hear this well-known actress from Hollywood speaking in front of all these people—not of her success, but of Jesus' achievements. In training as an actress, one always has to push oneself in order to achieve one's goals, but Dale had realized that nothing was as important in life as what you did with Christ and whether He was Lord of your life.

Then Billy Graham got up to speak. So this was the American who had come to tell the British about religion! I settled myself in my seat ready to analyze his performance and to collect some witticisms to share with my friends on the drive home.

But God had other plans.

As I sat and listened to Dr. Graham, I was struck by his sincerity. Even if I did not at first agree with him, I believed he was sincere. But what was he saying about a personal Saviour? I had been brought up in the church, but had never thought about Jesus being a personal Saviour. In my belief, the Jesus who had hung and suffered until death upon a cross had died for the whole world.

Then Billy said, "If you had been the only one on this earth, Jesus would have been willing to die for you—only He was pure enough to be sacrificed for your sins. God loved you so much that He sent His only Son to die for you. All *you* have to do is to realize your need, acknowledge your sin, and ask Him to come into your life."

Was this oversimplifying the Bible?

I thought of what I had been taught as a child. It *was* simple the way Miss Godfrey, my primary school Headmistress, had taught the Scriptures. I had loved to listen to her as she had told about the teachings and life of Christ. Had I missed the significance of God's love in my quest for happiness and self-satisfaction?

"For what shall it profit a man if he shall gain the whole world and lose his own soul? How many people here tonight have no time for God because of their ambition for material things?"

Wow! That was a blow right between the eyes. He was getting personal now.

For me, knowledge of Jesus Christ had been enough. When I left school I remember thinking, "I've got to get on in this world; if people know that I believe in God, maybe it will stop me getting on in some circles—so I will keep it to myself." How selfish. I had wanted to take all of God's blessings, but I had been ashamed of His Son. In that moment, as Billy Graham spoke, I realized that I was indeed a sinner who needed Jesus so much.

"But seek ye first the kingdom of God, and his righteousness; and all these things shall be added unto you." Billy Graham quoted from Matthew 6:33.

Oh, God, I have not put You first in my life. It has all been self-seeking.

I had laughed at the words *saved* and *sinner*. Now here I was confronted with Christ. Not the One whom I had seen hanging on a cross in a beautiful Renaissance painting—but a living Redeemer.

"There are many who believe suicide to be the answer to their problems!"

Had John Mercer told Billy Graham about me? He worked for Lloyds of London who were insuring the Crusade, but surely John did not know my secret thoughts of the past weeks. Did they show in my face? I glanced quickly at John, but there didn't seem to be any clue by his expression.

"You cannot run away from your problems. But by coming to the foot of the cross and realizing your need of forgiveness, you can find peace that passeth all understanding through accepting Christ."

Peace. How I had longed for peace and looked for it in so many ways. Always wanting to find the answer to life, wanting to belong. Needing to be understood. What a terrible mess I had made of this life that God had given to me! I had even thought about ending it. *Lord, forgive me.* But I don't have the courage to face it any more alone. I want to give my life to You, but I'm so terribly afraid of what these friends will think. *Dear God, give me the courage to turn this life over to You.*

I sat there praying and watching the crowds go towards the platform to give their lives to Christ. And there I sat—held back by thoughts of being laughed at by my friends. But I continued to pray; and then it seemed I realized that important as it was what my friends thought of me, it was far more important what God thought of me. Suddenly, I felt myself stand! God had given me the courage to make this decision, and I stepped out into the aisle!

Dale Evans's voice came back to me as I remembered her telling what Christ meant to her, and I thought, "For the first time in my life, I'm not ashamed to let others know I believe in Jesus Christ."

11

"You started on the Great Quest the moment you were born....Searching for something you never had....At the loneliest moments in your life, you have looked at other men and women and wondered if they too were seeking— seeking something they couldn't describe but knew they wanted and needed."

Peace With God
BILLY GRAHAM

It is hard to conceive that, due to a childlike response to an invitation to accept Christ as Saviour, there could be such a drastic change in my life.

Yet, this is exactly what happened.

That night at Harringay Arena in London as I stood by the platform along with so many others, I had finally reached a decision. I was no longer tossed in my mind as to what the future held. I had reached a point of no return, for this transaction was with God.

I had simply given everything over to Christ—all my heartaches, longings, and ambitions. Uppermost in my mind was the realization that everything had been self-seeking in my life. Now, instead of always comparing myself with others, my yardstick of perfection was Jesus. His selfless life made mine utterly contemptible. But I was also tremendously aware of the magnitude of His love.

There was now a light at the end of the tunnel.

I had felt compelled to answer an invitation that Billy Graham had given. I—who had always tried to hide any feelings of need from my friends—was now standing before an audience of twelve thousand people attesting to the fact that I did need Someone.

My mind was blurred from the drugs, but there were very vivid thoughts that whirled at breakneck speed through my befuddled brain.

"My friends—what can I say to them? Maybe I can slip away and no one will notice me."

The crowd that had come forward was now being escorted out of the Arena to a destination unknown.

We passed through nondescript halls until we were ushered into a large room. I could see people were beginning to sit and talk, and that was the last thing I wanted to do. I did not want to discuss what I had done with anyone, so I gradually edged my way to the back of the room, making a slow beeline for the exit.

"No one will notice," I thought.

But alas, I was spotted. Out of the corner of my eye I saw a lady (complete with Bible) approaching me.

"Trapped," I mused. "I don't want to talk to anyone." A fear enveloped me—again not wanting people to know of my need.

Perhaps you have had the joy of meeting someone for a few moments only, yet you feel as if they care and understand. As I turned in acknowledgment of her greeting, I sensed that here was a person who did indeed care.

Her face had an openness of expression. I can only say that my first thoughts were, "What a truly beautiful woman! She has such an aura of serenity. How I long for this."

Her dark hair was styled in a pageboy. She was simply, but elegantly, dressed in a camel-colored coat. She talked to me for a while, but my mind was racing again.

"I must not let her know how I really feel...."

She read from the Bible and prayed with me, but all I could remember from our conversation was, "Don't forget, Joan, you don't walk out of here alone—Christ goes with you!"

The reassurance of these words lived with me, and I was to find they were inexplicably true. But at that moment I merely could cling to them like a child clings to a security blanket—afraid that someone, or something, will take it away.

The lady in the camel-colored coat was talking to me again. "Would you like to meet my husband?"

I nodded assent and followed her. Most of the crowds had dispersed. I wondered why she wanted me to meet her husband. My mind was beginning to play tricks on me. I didn't trust my speech as the phenobarbital was wearing off, and I did not want to stutter.

We arrived at an unmarked door; after knocking, she opened it to reveal a small dressing room. To my surprise, the occupant was Billy Graham! Ruth, his wife, explained what had happened. He was so enthusiastic and proceeded to say how delighted he was about my decision.

"This is great!"

I was so overwhelmed that all I could say in reply to his questions was an occasional, "Yes—no—yes—no."

It was several years later that Ruth told me Billy had asked her that night, "Do you *really* think we got through to that girl?"

I met my group of friends, and we drove home. I do not remember a word being spoken, but if there was any conversation, I was oblivious to it.

Thanking them, I got out of the car and entered the large Edwardian house where I had an apartment. My thoughts were manifold as I walked through the familiar rooms.

Something had happened in my life. Ruth Graham had said I was no longer alone—Christ was with me.

I hunted for the dark-red Bible my father had given me so many years ago and began to read—as if for the first time.

Familiar passages were read over and over.

"Behold I am with you...."

"Blessed are the poor in spirit...."

"For God so loved the world...."

Sitting in the same armchair that had been the scene of many hopeless depressions, I felt His presence with me and rejoiced in my heart that no longer was my life filled with despair.

First of all, I decided, with God's help I was going to change many situations.

I would move from this place and all of its lonely, unhappy memories.

I would, once and for all, end the relationship with John that was only tearing both of us apart.

These resolutions having been made, I fell asleep that night with my mind full of questions. But for the first time in years I had hope.

The next morning dawned; it was a typical late March, hazy, cold, London morning. But my first thoughts were of Christ. I knew He was with me! I determined to begin looking for a new apartment in which to start my new life.

Dressing hastily, I then read the want ads in the *Daily Telegraph*. There seemed to be several apartments available, and I called to make appointments.

The day was spent viewing prospective apartments. I finally settled on one in Kensington, near to the Royal Albert Hall and only a short walk from Kensington Gardens which I loved. I knew I could be happy there.

I was worn out that night when I returned to face the old apartment, but there was a feeling of accomplishment. The inevitable packing began, as I could not wait to get out of the depressing atmosphere. I had not taken any phenobarbital that day, but my body was so used to it that by bedtime it seemed every nerve was jumping. I reached for a sleeping pill to dull my senses and sank into the never-never land I had become accustomed to.

Now came the decision to tell John it was definitely all over. I struggled desperately to tell him it was finished, but no courage seemed to come.

What had I done? There had been no real change in my life!

A simple act of walking forward to stand at a platform could not transform me. Perhaps momentarily—but I was still the same.

I suddenly began to cry as the hopelessness of my life started to crowd in again. But even then I found myself praying!

"Dear Lord, if You really care, help me now! I'm sinking back again. Maybe it was a mistake to plan to move from here and then to face the devastating upset of finishing past relationships."

Reaching into my handbag for a tissue, I came across a small packet of Bible verses Ruth Graham had given me that night at the Crusade. I had thought they were fine for somebody else, but not for me, and had promptly forgotten them. But now I found myself looking at them.

Ruth had said, "Memorize these, Joan, they will help you grow stronger in Christ."

I looked at them hoping for some kind of strength, and I came to 1 Corinthians 10:13:

There hath no temptation taken you but such as is common to man: but God is faithful, who will not suffer you to be tempted above that ye are able; but will with the temptation also make a way to escape, that ye may be able to bear it.

"Oh, God,—You've promised—You've promised! You said You'd be faithful and not let me be tempted more than I can bear. Please help me now. I want to slide back—it's easier, Lord. Even in the unhappiness there was a feeling of just being able to sink into oblivion. Now I don't seem to have the strength again to change my life. God, I believe You will make a way to escape, only right now I am sinking—wanting to take the easy way out."

I began to memorize the verse as I packed. I who would have laughed at the idea a few days ago, now was asking God to help me resist the temptation of taking the easy way out. But it was hard, so hard.

Moving day came and I forced myself to keep going. Once moved in, I felt a tremendous sense of joy come over me, and I danced—the only expression that came naturally to me at that moment. David had danced before the Lord. I danced from room to room of my new home, praising Him and thanking Him for the release that had flooded through me.

I passed Hyde Park Corner that day. The daffodils never had looked more beautiful to me. Someone had said, "From now on you will never look at the world in quite the same way," and it was true.

I began to find I could put my life in perspective now. Always before, my thinking had been colored by what *I* wanted to achieve. My horizons had been "boxed in," and there was no room for eternal values. Eternity loomed before me. Life was to be lived each day with that in mind. But it was not a subject to be dreaded, for I read Jesus' promises in the Bible of the joy that awaited us with Him.

One day however, after having unsuccessfully auditioned for a play, I came back to my apartment tired and feeling depressed. I was still on a see-saw as far as my emotions were concerned. Opening the front door, I noticed that a small parcel addressed to me was lying on the mat. Tearing the wrapper off, I discovered a book entitled *Peace With God,* by Billy Graham. There was also a note from Ruth saying she hoped I would enjoy it and asking me to call her and have tea.

I was deeply impressed that she had taken the time to send the book to me. Her note cheered me and made me realize again that here was a person who really cared. God had used her again in my life, just when I needed a touch of His love.

I went to bed early that night and began to read *Peace With God.* In the early morning I awakened—the book was still open and two-thirds of it read. There were so many answers there to questions I had had for so long as to *why* I was here. Suddenly the finiteness of my life took new meaning. This body that I move around in is going to die one day; but the *real me,* the me that loves, feels deep longings that cannot be put into words—that me will live on. By Christ's sacrifice on the cross, I will be deemed worthy to enter heaven; and *only* through Christ, for there is nothing we can achieve on this earth that can make us worthy. The joy of knowing this seemed to flood through me, as I thought of all there was to look forward to.

I hastily picked up the phone and dialed a familiar number, that of a friend with whom I had appeared in a TV series. A very platonic friendship had developed, and it was always good to be with him, because he made me laugh. Now as I told him what had happened in my life—I made *him* laugh.

"Joan, you are a character. Always trying something new. Next you'll be telling me you are banging a drum for the Salvation Army!"

Finally, laughing so hard, he told me he would have to call me back after he got control of himself. I put the telephone down and felt that I was an absolute failure as a Christian. "Well, Lord," I said to myself, "at least I made him laugh." But the "old" me was hurt. I hated the thought of being laughed at, criticized. It was so much easier to go with the crowd.

Looking at *Peace With God,* I remembered Ruth's note inviting me to tea. I dialed the number of the hotel and asked for her room number. Imagine my confusion when Billy Graham answered. Again he was so enthusiastic and delighted about my decision for Christ. Again all I could say was, "Yes—no—yes—no!" Ruth came on the phone, and we made arrangements to have tea at the hotel the next day. I looked forward to seeing her again.

Next day I was a little early for my appointment, so I decided to just wait in the hotel lobby, unobtrusively watching people come and go. The lobby was a marvelous place for an actress to study the mannerisms of the unsuspecting guests as they made their entrances and exits.

Little did I know that I was the object of observation. A young, attractive girl approached me and said, "Hi, I'm Leila. Aren't you Joan Winmill? Why, I have really been praying for you!"

This just shook me to the core. To think that this girl, whom I had never met, would be praying for *me.* I was deeply touched and thanked her. She explained that she was working with the Billy Graham Team as a Counselor with the women and was loving her stay in London. I immediately felt from her the same warmth and genuine concern that Ruth had shown when I had met her. To see this young, very attractive American girl talking without embarrassment about praying for someone, and to hear her express her faith in Christ was quite a revelation to this high Anglican who found it difficult to express her faith to anyone. (It would be even more so, after the conversation I had had on the telephone with my friend the day before.) Meeting Leila was to be an experience I would never forget, and over the years her friendship meant so much to me. Later when we were both married, we had yet another bond in Christ; our firstborn sons arrived on the same day, and we often celebrated their mutual birthdays.

Leila is now with her Lord. She died from cancer, leaving a beautiful family. I can remember how her husband, Doug Sparks, had to go on so many journeys, for his work with the Navigators kept him traveling constantly. Leila confided to me one day how she would long for his return. Now she has gone ahead of him on that awesome journey we must all take one day. She was unafraid, because she knew her destination.

Tea that afternoon with Ruth was a time of listening to a person who was so in contact with Christ. I had never met people like this before who could talk so naturally about Him. He seemed to fill her whole life.

Ruth and I prayed together. I sensed that even though there was still so much to be changed in my life, He was listening and would continue to guide me. Then Ruth gave me a real leather Bible, inscribed from her and Billy in this manner:

To Joan Winmill—God bless you. Billy Graham

"Being confident of this very thing, that He which hath begun a good work in you will perform it until the day of Jesus Christ." Philippians 1:6

We love you, Joan, and will be holding you up in our prayers. Ruth Graham

"Now unto Him that is able to keep you from falling, and to present you faultless before the presence of His glory with exceeding joy." Jude 24

I was deeply touched and could not find words to express all that I felt. The gift of *Peace With God* had moved me deeply and now this, too. I thanked her and wished that my English reticence could be swept aside to tell all that was in my heart.

Years later, Ruth told me that the day before I came to tea, she had felt she should go home, as she said she really wasn't being too much help to anyone. Billy was so busy with the Crusade, and she kept thinking of her children back in Montreat, North Carolina, and felt so homesick for them. Then I called and arranged to have tea with her, and she received a letter from another girl whom she was able to help. It often seems to happen in our lives that just when we feel we are not needed, the Lord says, "Wait, I have a few lambs who need you. Love them through Me."

Ruth's love and understanding that day held immeasurable value for my life. I do know that He had her there at a time when I so desperately needed the love of a fellow Christian; and He sent one who had walked many miles with Him and knew He did not let you down, no matter what the circumstances.

I left the hotel feeling stronger and taller. I returned to my new apartment with a new red Bible under my arm just burning to be read. Which is exactly what I did do as soon as I reached home. The print was readable, not like the usual Bible I had been used to, and I read avidly for hours, underlining verses that seemed to leap out at me, demanding my attention.

There was the question of going back to church again now, and I decided I would put that off for a long time. I did not want personalities or theology to spoil this newfound personal experience I had found with Christ. Ruth sensed this and encouraged me to find a church where I could be happy.

I'll never forget what happened to me one Sunday morning in April. I awakened and had the tremendous urge to go to church— it was the Holy Spirit working in me, giving me the desire. I did not have to force myself to go—I wanted to go and worship Him!

"I was glad when they said unto me, Let us go into the house of the Lord" (Psalms 122:1). Oh, David had put into words what was in my heart as I walked down the Brompton Road, passed Harrods, and approached the beautiful Anglican church of St. Margaret's.

When I walked in, the choir was singing a glorious anthem praising God. The whole church resounded to the voices and the magnificent organ. I felt transported out of my everyday feelings into a closer relationship of worship with Christ.

The Creed took on new meaning. "I believe in God the Father Almighty and in His Son, Jesus Christ our Lord." *He was my Lord now*. I had given this life over to Him. Here, in the beauty of this majestic edifice which had been built to glorify God, I sat like a small child who had suddenly been given all that her heart desired. To be loved like this by God, who had cared enough to send His Son to die for my sins, was at once exalting and humbling. I felt so unworthy, and yet I was bathed in a love that could only come from God.

My apartment now became the meeting place for a weekly Bible-study group. The Crusade organizers gathered together some of those who had made decisions and were anxious to learn more of this newfound life in Christ. We started with eight, and the numbers grew so quickly. I knew why the Lord had provided me with a large living room!

My Bible became dog-eared, because I marked it and studied it daily. This "dry book" now came alive each time I picked it up. It was not dead but alive to today's problems. I still have the Bible Billy and Ruth gave me, and I treasure each worn page. Some of them are patched together with Scotch tape, as I have read over and over again this love story from God.

John and I were growing further and further apart, and I longed for him to be able to find this joy I now had, but he could not stand to have me talk about Christ. I had changed so much since finding Him and was no longer clinging to someone simply out of the fear of being lonely. I prayed so much that John would come to know Christ. Perhaps in his finding Him we could have a life together. But it was not to be, for God had other plans for both of us. Sometimes there has to be a parting in our lives to make us completely dependent on God. Friends did not understand. They thought I considered myself too good for him. John did not understand; and even now, it is difficult to put down in words all that happened. But I continued to pray that God would work out this heartbreaking problem.

12

One morning the telephone rang early; it was Len Reeves, the producer of the commercial I had done for Silvikrin shampoo. He asked me to read for a part in a film he was working on for Billy Graham. I was really surprised and rushed around wondering just what I would wear. The telephone rang again. This time it was my agent saying he wanted me to go in an hour and audition for a part as a prostitute. I *really* wondered how I should dress now! I would not have time to get home to change before having to meet the director of the Billy Graham film, and the roles were obviously going to be poles apart. I decided to rely on lots of jewelry for the prostitute and discard most of it for the spiritual part!

I read for the prostitute and did not feel as if I had gone over too well. Maybe I needed more than jewelry to get me the part. Then I rushed over to the hotel to audition for Billy Graham's director, Dick Ross.

Looking back, I am amazed they had the faith to listen to me, for I had a very bad attack of sinus and talked as if I had adenoids. I kept assuring them I did not usually speak like this. When I started reading the script, I saw so much of my own life in it, I wondered if they had been spying on me!

Apparently they had cast most of the movie, but could not find the right girl to play the leading role. It was the story of an actress who, after much searching and heartache, comes to know Christ through a Billy Graham Crusade! Later I learned that when Dick Ross was talking to Ruth Graham about the role, she had said, "Why I counseled an actress the other night. Wouldn't it be interesting to have someone who had actually been converted to Christ through Bill's meetings play the role?"

When Dick Ross told me I had the part, my first feeling was of complete unworthiness because there was so much still wrong in my life. But I was assured that they wanted me to play Ann Woodbridge in *Souls in Conflict*. It was to be the start of a wonderful association with Dick Ross and, later, his wife Wanda. They have been, and continue to be, very close friends in Christ.

Appearing also in the film was a beautiful American actress Colleen Townsend, who had married Louis Evans, Jr. "Coke" had been a starlet in Hollywood; when Christ came into her life she decided a movie career was not for her. She married Louis and they were living in Scotland while he studied for his divinity degree.

Working with her was heartwarming experience. She helped this bewildered, new Christian in so many ways by her gentleness of spirit and completely natural attitude towards others. I watched her life very closely. Coke has since written the books *A New Joy* and *Love Is an Everyday Thing*. She completely radiates joy and love in her own life.

After finishing the shooting of the film, it was time for the Billy Graham team, Dick Ross, and Coke to go back to America. I missed them all, since I felt as if I had known them all my life. There was still so much to learn of this new Christian road that I was now journeying on. It seemed I stumbled so many times and wanted to say, "I'll never make it. The Lord is going to get so tired of my making so many stupid mistakes!"

The evening Bible classes kept me going from week to week. *Bible classes!* Just the words made me want to laugh when I thought of how opposed I had always been to anything organized, as far as religion was concerned. Now I was actually having Christians meet in my apartment!

I was offered the leading role in *The Little Hut,* which would be touring England. I jumped at the part without reading the script as it would be good publicity for me. I shall never forget one Thursday night when I told the Bible group I would not be able to be with them. I had to read through the play for the following day. I sat in the next room looking over my part for the first time. The script was new and crisp, and just the feel of it in my hands excited me.

As I read it, I suddenly realized it would be considered risque by many Christians. (Though by today's standards it would probably pass as family entertainment.) It was the story of three people shipwrecked on an island—a wife, her husband, and her lover. I could just imagine all the criticism that would come my way. By now, I had received a great deal of publicity in the newspapers concerning my conversion. Then it hit me! What really counted was what it would do to my relationship with the Lord. Would *He* condemn my being in the play?

I asked to be released from my contract. The answer was no, as the publicity for the show was already out. I can only tell you that I learned my lines without giving thought to them. (I delivered one long monologue looking blankly out into the audience.) Somehow I got the best reviews I have ever received—it was ironic. I also got some pretty hot mail too, from Christians.

"Call yourself a Christian? How dare you be in such a disgusting play! You are a disgrace to the Lord!"

This made me feel unbelievably low. I read my Bible in the dressing room and asked the Lord for *His* guidance. I waited and nothing seemed to happen in response to that prayer.

We continued to tour with the play and reached Cardiff, Wales. On Saturday evening after the final show in that city, I was in my dressing room taking off my makeup and there was a knock on the door. Calling out, "Come in," I turned to see a grinning young man with tousled hair standing there.

"What a story! BILLY GRAHAM CONVERT IN LEWD PLAY! How do you do. I'm a reporter with the local newspaper."

My heart sank as I asked him to sit down. *Lord, You've got to give me the right words to say.* The silent prayer went up as I sat smiling at this young man and sizing him up (while he did the same with me).

"I'd much rather you didn't, you know. I really don't need that kind of publicity right now."

"But I can't pass up a story like this," he said. "It will be great!"

Desperately I poured out my heart to this young man, telling him all that the Lord had done in my life. As a new Christian I was still floundering; perhaps it had been wrong to take this part, but I still had so much to learn.

He listened, then said, "It's all very interesting, but I do have a job to do."

"All right," I said, "I'll give you an interview if you promise me one thing."

"That's a deal," he said.

"Come with me to church tomorrow morning." He looked completely flabbergasted for a moment and then smilingly agreed.

We met the next day and went to a beautiful old church for the eleven o'clock service. The service was long, but inspiring, and the Welsh voices completely transported me.

As we came out of the church into the bright sunlight he turned, shook my hand, and said, "You can forget about the story." During the service God had spoken to him in the quietness of his heart. I silently thought, *Thank You, Lord*.

Through this experience I learned two things. First, when you make a mistake, God does hear and helps you if the cry comes from a contrite heart. Second, if I intended to follow Him, I was going to have to be more discerning in the parts that I accepted from now on.

"But, Lord, I may starve. So please help me. Do You want me to give up my career and go into Christian work? I feel so confused. But again You have promised to take care of me and I thank You for that." I had read in the New Testament what He had promised in Matthew 6:31-33:

Therefore take no thought, saying, What shall we eat? or, What shall we drink? or, Wherewithall shall we be clothed? (For after all these things do the Gentiles seek:) for your heavenly Father knoweth that ye have need of all these things. But seek ye first the kingdom of God, and his righteousness; and all these things shall be added unto you.

How lovingly He was telling me to trust Him. I was given unsolicited advice by some Christians (sometimes I thought they felt they were called to the "Grand Calling of Exhorters" and nothing else). What I really needed at this stage in my Christian life was love and understanding, and being pointed again and again to His Word. But—lovingly.

Each time I had asked Ruth Graham for advice she would say, "Why don't you ask the Lord to show you what you should do? Read the Bible and ask Him to enlighten you through His Word."

This made me want to read the Bible more and more. Each time I did this, a verse I had read would keep nagging me all day. I would know then that it was God's way of talking to me about my problem. Matthew 6:33 reminds one, "But seek ye first the kingdom of God...." Was I seeking God's will for my life, or was I still holding on to both worlds? I searched my heart, not knowing if I *was* completely in His will.

Arriving back in London after the finish of the tour, I collapsed in my apartment and tried to sort everything out. Then came the invitation to go to America for personal appearances with *Souls in Conflict*. I was dumbfounded! It would mean traveling all over America, speaking before thousands of people. Speaking—this terrified me! In the past I had always appeared behind the cover of another character, shielded by the author's words, not mine. I accepted, regardless of my uncertainties, and began to pack for the new adventure. This surely was an answer to my prayer concerning my future. It was the next step He wanted me to take, and I could never have taken it without Him.

When the time came for landing in New York, I eagerly craned my neck to see my first glimpse of America. I could hardly believe I was actually going to see this country which I had read so much about and had already grown to love.

13

As the skyline of New York came into view, I looked down at those famous buildings looming below. They seemed like huge, silent sentinels waiting to greet me. The plane landed; as the doors opened, a gust of hot air blew into the passenger area—it was 96 degrees and the humidity was 100 percent. Here I was dressed for winter in the same red coat I had worn to hear Billy Graham at Harringay, a black wool suit, and to top it off a Garbo-style white felt hat. It was Indian summer!

Everything looked so different from London—the cars, the people, the buildings. I really felt like a foreigner even though I spoke the same language. In the distance I could see some people waiting at the barrier. I thought one was Cliff Barrows, Billy Graham's song leader. Getting closer, I realized the person was not Cliff, but someone who could easily be mistaken for his brother. He put out his hand and said, "Hi! I'm Bill Brown—welcome to America!"

There was something in that greeting that made me take a long look at this handsome, virile American. Bill was working for the Billy Graham film ministry and was in charge of the premieres on the East Coast. With him was Walter Smyth, his boss, and together they took me to my hotel overlooking Central Park. During lunch Dr. Smyth briefed me on my New York schedule. The world premiere of the movie was to take place the following night at Carnegie Hall. I knew I would have to speak—the Lord would really have to give me the words to say, as I felt so totally inadequate.

Next day I sat on the platform at Carnegie Hall and thought of all the great artists who had performed there—which did not help my feelings of inadequacy one bit. In fact, it made me feel even more insignificant. I prayed to the Lord, "Please, Lord, just help me to say the right thing. I don't want to let You down."

When my turn came to speak, I simply tried to tell the audience what the film had meant to me during the making of it. I also told of how the Lord had helped me through some extremely difficult days when His love and grace had given me the strength I needed. In giving my life to Him I had accepted the gift of eternal life through Jesus Christ; I felt unworthy, yet He had forgiven and forgotten the past.

I sat down and hoped no one could see my knees shaking. Then the lights went down and the film was presented. I could not imagine how people would respond to Christ through a motion picture and was amazed as I watched the reaction to it. Invited to accept Him at the end of the film, scores of people stood up and came forward, just as I had done at the Crusade. It was the same message, only on film, and God used His Word to reach these people.

I was elated and overjoyed to think the film had met with this kind of response. Everyone I spoke with afterwards was delighted, and I was sailing on cloud nine—until a little old lady came up to me, shaking her fist in my face!

"Go back to England where you belong!" she said. "You've only come over here for the money—just like the English!"

If only she knew! At that moment I would willingly have gotten on the next plane out, for another lady was also waiting to pounce on me.

"Don't cross your legs when you are on the platform. Looks disgusting!"

I reeled as I listened to the two of them tear me apart, thanked them with a plastic smile, and returned to Bill Brown and company a little amazed by the heated criticism.

The days ahead were exciting ones. I traveled all over the States; everywhere I was met at the airport by a large entourage, whisked into a car, and taken through the city. Whereupon I was shown all the sights, taken to a hotel where I rested, and then appeared on TV and radio, plus which I was interviewed by the press. Then came the film showings at night.

In Nashville I almost died of embarrassment. At the airport to greet me was Pek Gunn, a dedicated layman; his wife, Frances; and a large contingent of police cars. I had never been in a police car before and felt like a criminal as we raced through town, sirens screaming all the way, to the Governor's for tea.

Upon my arrival in Houston, Texas, I met the Carloss Morris family.

Mrs. Morris, Senior, arranged to show me the interesting sights of Houston. I was instantly drawn to this delightful lady.

After we had visited some of the usual tourist stops, she turned to me and said, "Joan, there's someone I want you to meet who will be able to help you in the future."

She leaned forward and instructed her chauffeur to take us to a certain address. Looking out of the window of the car, I noticed we were leaving the affluent part of town and entering the poorer section. The car stopped outside a little frame house. I wondered, "Is this where the person lives who is supposed to help me?" It proved to be the highlight of my stay in Houston. Living in that little house was a lady who had been bedridden for many years, but one who had a radiance about her which I will remember always. Anyone entering her bedroom could sense that here was someone who knew the comfort of the living Christ. Mrs. Morris and I prayed with her and talked with her briefly. I needed to meet that lady, as the accolades and attention I was receiving had begun to go to my head.

On our way back to the hotel, Mrs. Morris said to me, "Joan, it's easy to serve Him when everything is going just right. But the true test comes when you are alone with Him day after day on a bed of pain, or are just simply facing life's everyday problems." I have remembered her words so many times because the years that lay ahead brought their share of problems. I found the same Christ, who sustained that little lady in her confined room, was there to help me too.

Our next stop on the tour with the film was to be Hollywood. I could hardly wait to see this Golden City with all the glamour it held. But I was to experience some unpleasant surprises. John had gone to the press in England and said I was a modern Joan of Arc, who was being sacrificed at the stake for the sake of the Billy Graham organization. The statement made all the London papers, and I panicked inside. The phone rang constantly in my room. Reporters from *Newsweek, The New York Times,* and other papers from all over the country were now asking for interviews. An overseas reporter from the English newspaper, *The Daily Express,* called me. He wanted an explanation of why I had been sacrificed "at the stake" like Joan of Arc. I told him I had not been coerced into anything, but was here of my own free will. He still wanted to see me and would be flying out the next day.

Newspapers across America carried major stories, and even *Newsweek* had a photo of me, along with the incredible news item of my "sacrifice." Angry reporters were invited to the house of Lionel Mayell in Altadena, where I was scheduled to speak the next night. (Imagine speaking when a *Daily Express* reporter is sitting in the front row!) Before opening my mouth I silently prayed, "Lord, give me the words. You can do it. I am just going to be depending on that verse in Philippians, 'I can do all things through Christ which strengtheneth me.' " (*See* 4:13.)

At the close of my testimony and talk, the *Daily Express* gentleman shook my hand and said, "You don't have to worry. The story will be a kind one."

The others said similar things. I can only say I thanked the Lord again that night for His love and protection. Some verses in Jeremiah gave me encouragement:

> Be not afraid of their faces: for I am with thee to deliver thee, saith the Lord. Then the Lord put forth his hand, and touched my mouth. And the Lord said unto me, Behold I have put my words in thy mouth.
>
> Jeremiah 1:8,9

These were the verses I clung to, as I spoke to so many thousands of people across America. Those words did not fail me as I spoke face-to-face with those who had come to judge in a living room in the Los Angeles suburbs.

Perhaps the highlight of my stay in Hollywood was visiting the home of Henrietta Mears, the lady dressed in bright colors whom I had seen on the platform at the Harringay Crusade in London. She welcomed me to her magnificent Bel Air home, but it was not the lovely surroundings that had me in awe. It was her gentle, loving way of talking to me about Jesus. As we sat and talked, I told her how worried I was as to what the Lord would have me do with my life—whether He wanted me to stay on in the theater and be a witness for Him there like Dale Evans, or whether He wanted me in full-time work for Him.

"First of all, a child of God should never be worried. Concerned maybe, but never worried, because He has your life completely in His hands and He is going to show you just what He wants you to do."

We prayed together. Then she opened her Bible and read me these words, "Commit thy way unto the Lord; trust also in him; and he shall bring it to pass" (Psalms 37:5).

"Joan," she said, "your lack of fully trusting Him makes me believe that you are holding back part of your heart for yourself and not completely letting God take over your life."

It was true. Being here in Hollywood and seeing all the familiar names of the studios still stirred my dreams of becoming an international star. But it *was* for myself and I was not kidding anyone.

Then together we prayed and turned all my ambitions over to Him. It was such a relief because my whole stay had been fraught with my own desires welling up inside me. I left Hollywood and headed back to the East Coast with a peace of mind concerning the future. I did not know what it was, but I simply was going to trust God from now on.

My next appearance was to be in Boston, Massachusetts, for seven days, and the Lord was really going to work fast there! Greeting me once more was Bill Brown, who had called me several times when I was in other cities. I was so glad to see him again and I just knew this was going to be a wonderful week.

Allan Emery, who was chairman of the arrangements for showing *Souls in Conflict,* and his lovely wife, Marian, made us feel very welcome. Several times we visited their beautiful suburban home. The role of Cupid was assigned to the Emery family. Between film showings and interviews, they always managed to get Bill and me together for some delightful tour of the city or for a drive along the beautiful shores of Massachusetts.

Bill and I never had time for a date, and the only way we could be alone was to meet behind the screen while the film was showing! We talked about our lives, our backgrounds, and what our aspirations and dreams were. All the time I felt a certain glow that I had never really known before.

One night I was praying in my room at the hotel, telling the Lord how happy I would be to be completely in His work if it was not His will that I should ever marry.

"But," I said, "if it is Your will, Lord, I surely would love to be married to someone like Bill Brown!"

Later that week, after the showing was over, Bill and I talked in the lobby of the hotel until well past midnight. We were the only ones left, apart from the night porter, but we still had so much to talk about. Bill was telling me all about his family.

He said, "My sisters have had so many boy friends propose, and I have heard them turn these guys down. I would hate to ask a girl to marry me and have her turn me down, as that would probably give me an inferiority complex for the rest of my life. If I *were* going to marry someone, I sure would like her to be like you."

With that, out of the blue, I impulsively said, "Why don't you practice on me?"

With that he asked me to marry him; from then on the memories are hazy, but I do remember saying, "Yes!" (To this day he still insists he was only practicing! Poor chap.)

He phoned his family in Philadelphia who advised him to "keep your feet on the ground, Billy!" They were concerned about his British actress sweeping their young brother off his feet. They really were justified in their caution, for we had only known each other for five weeks.

The next day was like a dream to both of us. Allan and Marian Emery were informed and were delighted. They could see what had been going on between us. I can remember sitting next to Bill at a banquet and nervously tearing the program to shreds before I knew what I had done!

The showing of the film in Boston was extended for another week, and we had seven more glorious days together. It seemed like a fairy-tale city to me and I did not care any more that the British had been defeated there. One Britisher had scored a victory and that was enough for me. We became engaged on November 11— Armistice Day!

Allan Emery took us to a jeweler where we chose a ring. Bill had very little savings, so Allan offered to make a loan with Bill paying him back gradually. It took several years of ten-dollar payments to pay for the ring. We were so grateful for Allan's kind gesture and the trust he had in us.

At the end of our stay I had to say goodbye to Bill, as we both had to go to separate cities with the film for a while. I flew to Washington. It was so hard to part. I could not take my eyes off the ring as I sat in the plane remembering all that had happened so very quickly. Henrietta Mears had told me to commit my way unto the Lord and trust in Him, and He would bring it to pass.

"I never dreamed it would be so quickly, dear Lord!"

Once in Washington, I was caught up again with all the arrangements for the premiere at Constitution Hall. That night, for the first time, I told publicly of my wanting to commit suicide. I had never mentioned it before, as I was afraid it would upset my family.

After the showing, a young man told me he had become so desperate with all the seemingly unsolvable problems in his life, he had decided to end it all that very night. Walking the streets, he had wandered into the showing. Hearing me tell of God's love in my life, how He had come in at a time when I was desperate too and thought suicide was the only answer, the young man decided to try again. He gave his life to the Lord. This incident was an answer to a prayer of mine, as I had wrestled with the fact of keeping my intended suicide a secret. The story reached the newspapers in England, and now everyone knew that Joan Winmill had once contemplated taking her life. I ached for my family but hoped they would understand. Some didn't, and it took many years to break down the barriers.

One night after a film showing, I had dinner with Bobby and Ethel Kennedy and Senator Henry Jackson. They were so interested in the film and what had happened to me. I found myself telling them everything that had transpired.

Ethel said, "How wonderful, you really feel that Christ is with you personally, wherever you go."

I assured her that this was so, and that now I knew I could count on Him whatever the circumstances in my life. The circumstances that were to come about in her life—the tragic and futile violence that would wipe out their happiness together—brought her even closer to the Lord, I know. Because of His grace she has been able to carry on so courageously. In Proverbs 31:10,11 we read, "Who can find a virtuous woman? for her price is far above rubies. The heart of her husband doth safely trust in her...."

Bobby found a virtuous wife and mother of his children in Ethel. I am thankful they enjoyed such happiness together, even though it was to be terminated so tragically. I am thankful too that Ethel has said she does not live without the hope of seeing him again.

Next on my agenda was a visit to Charlotte, North Carolina, where I would be staying in the home of Grady and Wilma Wilson. Grady had been a childhood friend of Billy Graham's and had traveled extensively with him as an Associate Evangelist. Grady met me at the airport and told me he had one stop to make before going home—the butcher's. He came out of the shop, grinning from ear to ear and carrying a big bundle of steaks.

"I've got you the biggest steak in the South," he said. "We'll barbecue it when we get home."

Since becoming engaged I had completely lost my appetite; I hoped I could eat this huge piece of meat that had been thrown on (what looked to me to be) a miniature bonfire.

We all sat down to eat, and I was dying to tell Grady and Wilma the news about Bill and me. I took one bite out of the steak—a piece of meat that, during the war, would have lasted our whole family a week. That bite was all I could eat because of Bill Brown, and I burst out the news to them.

Grady often regales me with this story of an English girl who toyed with the best steak in North Carolina because she was *in love!*

After my stay in Charlotte, I was invited to spend some time with Ruth Graham at Montreat. I rested there for a month before going on again to more showings. During that time I realized fully why the Lord had brought Ruth and Billy together. She was so exceptional. The children were very young, so she had five busy little souls, all clamoring for attention. Billy was away so much of the time. She was equipped to meet any of the situations that kept their warm, rustic Early American home in a state of perpetual motion. Children, dogs, visitors, and phones ringing caused this house to resound with the noises of sheer exuberant living.

Ruth gave me a room away from all the family noise. It was a chance to recuperate and learn some lessons in everyday living from a person who, in a completely unaffected way, had grown to know the joy of constant communion with the living Christ.

Of course, there were frequent knocks on my door and the children bounded in, clambered onto my bed, and asked me to read to them. They liked to listen to this lady with "the funny accent."

Ruth's quiet talks, by the log fire each night, were locked in the secret place of my heart until I would have need to remember their deeper meaning and realize their value. Her Bible seemed to be part of her, always open—waiting to be read—in whatever room she was.

"When the children were born," she said, "I found I could no longer set a certain hour for reading the Bible. I would get up earlier and earlier in the morning, but when I did there would always be a little one needing attention. So I decided to take my Bible with me wherever I was working and, if I were able to read a few verses at a time, I would still be guided and encouraged by His Word." When my own children came, I remembered this. I know now it was the secret to being able to have that quiet flow of communication with the Lord.

Ruth never gave the appearance of feeling sorry for herself because Billy was away so much, even though I know she missed him terribly. The only time I ever saw her a little down was one day when she read a letter from a missionary she had not heard from since her college days.

The letter read, "You probably don't remember me, Ruth, now that you are the wife of such a famous Evangelist. It must be a very glamorous life. My husband and I are stuck here in the mission field."

Ruth looked up and I saw a tear in her eye as she said, "At least she is with her husband." She put the letter away and quickly resumed her many tasks.

Bill flew down to see me and stayed at the local inn. I had told Ruth all about him, and she told me she was concerned that we really did not know each other very well. Then she saw his photograph and said, "Anyone who looks so much like Cliff Barrows has got to be all right!"

Bill made a hit with her immediately. The children adored him and delighted in spying on us. Bunny, who was very small, perceptively said (with thumb in mouth), "I think Uncle Bill *loves* Aunt Joan!"

Ruth lent us Billy's car and Montreat was a wonderful place to court. We drove through the beautiful mountains and forests, and my heart was so grateful to the Lord for all this happiness. I was sure I would just burst one day from sheer joy.

One night while parked by the entrance to Montreat, we were deep in discussion (or something) when a car pulled up behind us. It was the Montreat patrol car making a routine check. Bill started the engine up so fast and roared out of there! Later he said it must have looked terrible—Billy's car with another man in it. The patrol officer might have thought he was with Ruth! She laughed about it when we got home. Later that night, while reading my daily chapter of Proverbs, this verse caught my eye, "The wicked flee when no man pursueth...." (28:1).

Now the time came when I would meet Bill's family in Philadelphia. We flew back from Montreat together, as I was to appear with the film in that historic city of the Liberty Bell. They were all at the airport to greet us. I felt just like a buck private at his first drill session—really getting an inspection! Little Gayle, Bill's niece, listened to my accent for a moment and said, "Why does she talk Russian, Mom?"

At dinner that night around the family table, everyone talked; I would wait for an interval to be able to say something profound—to make a good impression—but there never was an interval, everyone kept right on! Bill told me afterwards that they thought I was rather quiet! My grandmother's training had always been that you waited until someone finished speaking before you chimed in. I have revised this teaching now and jump right in with all of them. It took a few years to get used to this vital family. I have grown to love them all. Then too, they have grown to love this English girl who always seems to go through life in low gear. (Compared to them!)

Film showings had been scheduled all over England and Scotland, so I had to fly back and leave Bill for a while. I have never understood why Shakespeare ever wrote "...parting is such sweet sorrow...." It was anything but sweet. At the airport Bill gave me a beautiful little compact with a music box in it which played "I Love You Truly." I loved it so much that I played it over and over until finally the mechanism slowed down and it sounded like "Short'nin' Bread."

Being in England again brought all the problems of my past back before me. The press continued to trail me. The weeks went by, and I was becoming a wreck from all the hounding. By the time I was to return to America, I left England distraught, overtired, and sad.

Daddy came to see me off and pressed a little box into my hand. "Open it when you are on the plane," he said. It was hard to say goodbye to him. Kissing him, I then turned and ran to the plane, feeling so torn inside. As my foot left English soil, I wondered when I would be back in this country I loved so much. Once I boarded the plane I sat praying for Daddy, for his health was always causing him pain and discomfort.

Remembering the little box I reached down into my handbag and unwrapped it carefully. Inside was a small, beautiful gold cross with a card written by Daddy. "Keep this remembrance of our Lord close to you. It will lessen the miles between us as we think how much He loves us both. Your everloving Daddy."

The tears that ran down my face as I looked out of the window were both tears of parting and tears of joy. Since I had become a Christian, Daddy had never been able to talk to me about the Lord. He had been so difficult to witness to because he was such a kind, gentle man, always helping others. He put me to shame. I had explained to him that because of our inherent sinful nature, none of us was worthy of God's love. He had listened and said, "I'm glad for you, dear, that you have found such peace through Him."

Then the subject would change; but now as I sat looking at the cross and the card, I knew it was his way of showing me that he had at last acknowledged his need, too, of our Lord. Perhaps in no other way would he have been able to express himself.

Upon my arrival back in the States, everything picked up momentum. I was to stay with Bill's sister, Eva, for a few days until I got my schedule. Bill had news that he was being transferred to the West Coast, and this would mean our being separated once more. We decided to be married immediately, so that I could be with him in California. The whole family went to work on this monumental project. It was Monday, and we made plans to be married Thursday evening.

I can hardly believe it, but in four days our church wedding was planned. Bill's mother flew up to Philadelphia from her home in Florida. For the first time I met this lady I had heard so much about from Bill. I knew right away why Bill loved and respected her, for even though she had suffered so many hardships, she always showed the love of Christ. Widowed, with six children in school, her complete dependence had been on her Saviour, who had given her comfort and strength through the years. She accepted me into her family with such love that I felt very privileged to be her daughter-in-law.

As a result of telephoning, there were over 200 people at the wedding! Then too, instead of cake and punch in a church basement, the guests were invited to a beautiful reception given for us in the lovely home of Fred and Millie Dienert. It was hard to believe how gracious these newfound Christian friends were to two bewildered, but desperately happy, people. I remember having to walk down that long aisle on my own. I missed my father's arm to lean on. How happy he would have been to see me married, but finances and the short notice made it impossible for him to be there.

As Bill and I took our vows, I realized the great solemnity of that moment. These were promises to God that we were making. Here we stood, two people from very different backgrounds, brought up thousands of miles apart, and yet all along God knew we would one day be led together and become one.

After the beautiful reception at the Dienerts' house, I had to go back and help Bill sort out his personal effects. He had not had time to even think of it, and here we were planning to leave for California shortly. In the middle of the packing, he remembered he had not phoned for a reservation at a hotel for that night. It was now two in the morning. When the hotel clerk answered the phone, he couldn't understand whether Bill wanted a room for the middle of that night or the next night! When we finally arrived at the hotel at four-thirty, we were weary people; except for my drooping orchid, I am sure the clerk never would have guessed that here was a honeymoon couple!

Two bleary-eyed people left for California the next morning. Each day we would try to travel over 500 miles. I can tell you—it was not the ideal way to spend a honeymoon!

We arrived in Los Angeles, and then there was the job of apartment hunting. After much searching we managed to find a little apartment in Van Nuys. It was not palatial by any means, but it was clean. We found the birdlike, white-haired landlady was in our apartment all the time, making sure we were being good tenants. A bang on the bathroom wall from her adjoining apartment would indicate she thought we had run enough bath water. After a while I began to feel she really lived with us, especially when we were told not to close any kitchen cabinets after ten o'clock (the noise kept her awake). There was wall-to-wall carpeting in the kitchen (the variety that seemed to eat up every stain). This had been put down so our footsteps wouldn't bother her. Each time Bill went out he slammed the screen door behind him; one day when we returned, the screen door had been taken off its hinges, and it was now open season for all the flies and mosquitoes to invade our house. The temperature that summer zoomed to 110 degrees for over a week.

Now we were living right next to Hollywood, and Bill was the film representative for the area. It sounded very glamorous to those back in England who would write saying, "Well, you finally made it. You are lucky, Joan!" Oh, how I longed for London, with its transportation. Stuck in the San Fernando Valley, not being able to drive, I had to rely on Bill for everything.

One day Bill opened the back door and called out, "I don't think you're going to like it, honey!" There he stood with the shortest crew cut I have ever seen. He was right—I didn't like it! It just did not look like the Bill Brown I had married. That chin my aunt had warned me about seemed to stick out even further. I could tell he was not crazy about the crew cut either. That night at a film showing he kept running his hand through the stubble—hoping it might have grown!

The apartment was so hot. We finally managed to get enough money to buy a small revolving fan from the Salvation Army Thrift Store. It wobbled precariously but at least helped move the air. Bill was earning very little money at this time, but it did not seem to worry us. We were happy together and could laugh at the ecccentricities of the landlady. One morning, thinking we had already left for church, she walked into our bedroom and was greeted by Bill in his birthday suit!

Bill would watch me cook and keep saying, "We just don't cook like that in America, honey!" We didn't in England either, but I had to learn somehow. It was mostly by trial and error that I began to bring a semblance of order to our little apartment and the meals I hesitatingly served. Bill luckily had been born with a cast-iron stomach.

I remember saying to Bill, "You know, I don't know how people stay married without the Lord, do you?"

"Surely it hasn't been that bad, has it?" he asked incredulously.

We laughed and thanked Him for being able to come to Him with all our problems, and too—with all our happiness together.

Due to my conservative English background, I had much to learn to accept of American life—especially when Bill would pull up in some little town outside of Los Angeles, roll down the window of the car, and yell, "Hey, buddy—where's the First Baptist Church?" This man was no more his buddy than the man in the moon!

Our time was spent at so many showings of *Souls in Conflict*. Bill sometimes booked us for twenty-nine screenings a month. It was heartening for me to see the Lord continue to work through this medium. Sometimes there were very small meetings, which contradicted critics who said it was the hypnosis of the large crowds that so often caused people to respond. It was that quiet, inner need that responded—that quiet need that is basically within everyone, if they will only acknowledge it.

It was during this time that we received some wonderful news. John had given his life to Christ at Wembley Stadium in London, during a Billy Graham Crusade there! Bill and I were overjoyed as we heard how God had worked. John, with reporters and photographers at hand, had been all set to punch Billy on the jaw, but instead Billy had reached out and shaken his hand! They were then able to sit and talk. John responded to Christ after seeing the sincerity of this man who had such a calling from God to tell others of the Gospel of Jesus Christ.

Recently Bill and I were asked to appear on a TV talk-show along with John, who now lives in America and travels all over the country with his own Christian drama group. On camera the three of us expressed our love for Christ.

As I look back on our lives, when John and I met we were two people with a longing in our souls that only God could satisfy. The turmoil and anguish that surrounded our relationship was really a cry for help and a deep desire to be loved.

I am glad that for many years John, too, has been *no longer alone*.

"I love little children and it is not a slight thing when they, who are fresh from God, love us."

CHARLES DICKENS

With my health record I did not seem to be a very good risk for motherhood. Two nervous breakdowns did not qualify me as a very suitable candidate for this responsible and arduous role. I loved children—but other people's. I did not want to be tied down to more responsibilities, especially when we were traveling around so much and not sure what our future held. Basically the nagging fear of my mother's death in childbirth haunted me.

Knowing how much Bill wanted a child, I began to really pray about it, pouring all my fears out to the Lord. It seems that each time there is an important step in my life I have to wrestle everything out with the Lord, and this time was no exception. But He answered my prayers, and recorded in my old red Bible are these words:

> October 6, 1955 I pray that if it is His will, soon we will have a child.
> "...Fear not...for thy prayer is heard...." Luke 1:13

July 16, 1956 William Frederick Brown, Jr., born.
"For this child I prayed; and the Lord hath given me my
petition which I asked of Him," 1 Samuel 1:27

November 22, 1959 David Stewart Brown born.
"Lo, children are an heritage of the Lord...." Psalms 127:3

What a heritage! These two sons have brought Bill and me such
joy, and continue to do so. Oh, there are times when I still wonder
if I shall ever make it as a mother and have to cry out to God to give
me wisdom to deal with the diverse problems. But I would not
change my role as a mother for anything else. The rewards are
manifold as those whose lives have been entrusted to you develop
into manhood and start the great adventure of life on their own.
Recalling my very real fears when I carried each of my sons brings
me closer to the Lord, as I see how well He took care of me.

Bill had decided it was time to leave California and head back
East, but our bank account did not agree. So we arranged to work
our way back by showing the film in some towns across the country. This sounded good in theory, but in practice it was another
matter!

We did not have enough money to stay at motels, so Bill thought
it a great idea to buy a trailer. I had seen luxurious trailers on sales
lots along the highway and imagined it would be fun to pull one.
However, the price tag for a modern trailer-home was way over our
heads. Bill said we would have to look for a used one in the local
want ads. I thought a used one wouldn't be bad if the owner had
taken good care of it.

My dear husband took me to a little trailer lot in the San Fernando Valley and showed me the trailer we *could* afford. I took one
look at it—priced at $110, it was a crate-on-wheels. Bill told me to
imagine how it would look after he had painted it. My imagination
didn't help. I envisioned a "repainted" crate-on-wheels. Inside was
even worse; the old gentleman living in it had not kept it up at all.
"The basics are there," said Bill, "and look, it has a closet, so we
can hang our clothes, and they won't get creased!" *The eternal op-*

A bridesmaid at four — in a dress
made by my grandmother.

The last photograph
of my dear mother.

One of the world's
most gentle men — my father.

Nanny, my grandmother, poses
in her "fancy dress" costume.

As Raina in the George Bernard
Shaw play, ARMS AND THE
MAN, with Andrew Crawford.

"Just Married" to Bill Brown.
(Editor's note: Bill is now the
President of World Wide
Pictures, and was the executive
producer for the highly-
successful motion picture,
THE HIDING PLACE.)

I look on as Tricia Nixon Cox greets Ethel Waters on the occasion of the celebration of her sixty years in show business.

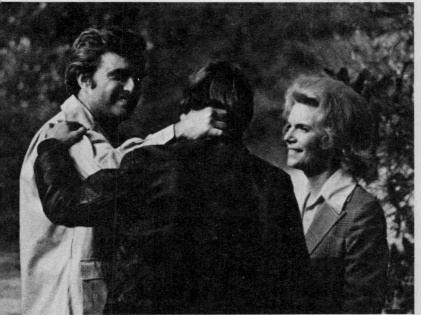

The final scene from TIME TO RUN, with Ed Nelson and Randall Carver.

Bill, David, and Bill, Jr., join me on our front doorstep in Sherman Oaks, California.

World Wide Pictures
presents

No Longer Alone

In Color

For Joan Winmill
the seeds of doubt
of loneliness...of
fear...were sown
at a very early age.
Before she reached
her teens, she had
experienced more
than her share of
heartache—
heartache that
plunged her into
this remarkable
story.

As a young child, Joan said
goodbye to her mother, who was
leaving to give birth to a second
child...

"It's just for a few days...and
I'll have a lovely surprise for you."

Joan looked longingly at her
mother as she got into the car,
not realizing that this goodbye
would be their last.

When Joan's grandmother received word of her mother's death, Joan was bustled off to an aunt's house. There, as Joan plays on a swing in the garden, voices drift out of an open window, and Joan begins to understand...

"Mummy has gone to be with the angels. Grandmother will take good care of you, Sunshine."

Her father's job took him on the road for long periods of time, but her grandmother managed to fill her hours with excitement.

Joan's favorite activity was a visit to the cinema...an activity that gave birth to her interest in acting.

But because of her grandmother's sudden nervous breakdown, Joan was forced to move again—this time to live with her aunt and her cousin, Stewart.

Once again, Joan was to experience a heartbreaking loss —for leukemia had claimed Stewart's young life.

"Don't cry, Joan. He's with God and with Mummy. She can take care of him."

During the time that Joan's father was making plans to remarry, Joan attended St. Hilda's School for Girls.

"I am truly sorry, Joan, that you've known so much sadness at your age. But God is greater than that . . . His love is greater than our tragedies."

It was here that Joan's interest in acting was encouraged, and she appeared in a number of school plays. It was also here that a sensitive headmistress, Miss Godfrey, gave Joan the patient understanding she so desperately needed.

Upon completion of her schooling, Joan found work as a secretary. But at the urging of her friends, she decided to try out for a part as an understudy in a play. And through a series of unusual events, Joan soon got the lead role in William Douglas Home's THE CHILTERN HUNDREDS, playing in London's famed West End.

A dashing young American's summer visit to London brought fresh sunshine to Joan's clouded life. Following a performance of THE CHILTERN HUNDREDS, Joan was introduced to an admiring fan, Robert Kennedy.

A whirlwind of happy times followed—rides in the country, visits to art galleries, quiet dinners for two, picnics at the beach, and sunsets that seemed to linger into the night.

But a letter from America shattered Joan's happiness:

"I know you'll be happy with me at some good news; I am getting married to Ethel Skakel..."

Looking back, Joan knows today that Ethel, a woman of great strength and understanding, was God's best for Bobby. But at the time, the pain was deep, and real, and...

From that moment on, it seemed as though Joan's career as a rising stage and screen actress was marred by an ever-growing darkness. Fearing a nervous breakdown, she began relying on pills to keep go

She began to forget her lines, stumbling through them while on stage or in front of cameras.

Her friend, Alan, notices the sudden change that's come over her.

"What's happening to you lately? You spend half your life in bed...avoiding all your so-called friends, refusing auditions or making a mess of the few you manage to drag yourself to..."

Alan's words seemed to cut right through her. It was more than she wanted to hear, because she knew it was the truth. Joan ran screaming from the restaurant, and climbed aboard a double-decker bus, make-up streaming down her face.

Once inside her apartment—a place that had now become a kind of shell for her, keeping others away—the thoughts of her next move raced through her mind. And the thought, the one thought, that kept coming back to her was to take her own life. Just turn on the gas and slip into a quiet, gentle sleep. No more pain. No more loneliness. No more never-ending darkness.

But God had other plans for Joan Winmill. A chance phone call, coming at the deepest point in her depression, brought her an invitation to attend Billy Graham's London Crusade.

"What could a loud American possibly tell the British about religion?" she wondered aloud.

That night, for the first time, she discovered what Miss Godfrey meant years earlier, when she told Joan, "His love is greater than all our tragedies."

timist, I thought, as I surveyed the cramped quarters which were going to be home for a few months. After we paid the elderly gentleman, he said, "Once you've lived in a trailer, you won't want to live anywhere else." I was not convinced.

Bill repainted the exterior and the interior. He got so carried away that he painted the inside of the icebox with the same paint he had used for the rest of the trailer; the result was that our food tasted and smelled of paint for the whole trip. Friends donated all kinds of accoutrements with which to furnish our new home, even making curtains, which helped considerably. As we left, the staff of World Wide Pictures, wives, and loved ones came to see us pull out of the parking lot in our vintage home on wheels. Someone remarked, "At least you're not pregnant, Joan." Guess what? I was!

To make things worse, on our first night out we befriended a stray dog, and had another traveling companion.

Bill had written ahead to towns in all the different states. In some states like New Mexico we were going around in circles, since we showed the film in such towns as Albuquerque, Tucumcari, and Alamogordo. With a cross-country schedule of three months, we had many miles to go, many showings to attend, and I was getting larger by the hour! Luckily, I had a pink tweed suit with a Chanel-type jacket, so I could hide the fact for a while. After holding my skirt together with a safety pin (which graduated in size each week), it finally became necessary to use a large mattress-pin to hold body and soul together! My legs were exceedingly swollen and looked like tree trunks. In one town, after I had been introduced to speak, I walked past a group of ladies and overheard one of them say, "My, doesn't she have an extraordinary figure for an actress!"

One day the trailer hitch broke as we were heading down the highway. Our dishes went flying, and the whole interior was a mess of dog food and our food. Bill said, "But, honey, our clothes are still hanging up in the closet." Oh, that closet, you would think it was the answer to everything!

The smell of the butane gas when I awakened in the morning with the usual sickness that goes with pregnancy was enough to make me throw up everything. (The smell of the stray dog and food didn't help, either.) Bill and I shared a bed that only measured thirty-nine inches across and was as hard as a board.

After the long trip I was thankful to arrive at Bill's mother's house in West Palm Beach. Mom took great care of me, and it was wonderful to rest after all those meetings. I bought a prenatal-care book and learned it was best not to travel while expecting! We had traveled 3,000 miles and there were quite a few to go before we could settle, so I chose to ignore these warnings.

We left the trailer with Bill's mother. She later was able to sell it for us to some gypsies at a handsome profit of fifty-five dollars. I was never so glad to get rid of any possession in my life. The words of the old gentleman, "Once you live in a trailer you'll never want to live anywhere else," have become part of our joking vocabulary.

Bill was loaned by Billy Graham to Howard Butt, the popular businessman-evangelist, for several months so he could help set up Crusades in the South. We lived in Macon, Georgia, then Greensboro, North Carolina, and finally Montgomery, Alabama, where I could now await the birth of my first child. We rented a furnished home there. While Bill raced around making arrangements for another Crusade, I poked around, looking like a laden barge, preparing clothes for the imminent arrival of our baby.

The baby did not choose to make an appearance at the prophesied time. After three extra weeks of waiting, the doctor decided that it was time to induce the birth. I was to awaken at six the next morning, take a large bottle of castor oil immediately, then enter the hospital. When the alarm went off, and I saw the bottle of castor oil awaiting me, I groaned. I did not want to face this day, but if there is one thing that having a baby teaches you—you cannot run away. It is inevitable that something will have to happen!

I arrived at the hospital, kissed Bill goodbye (as he was due on a radio program and had a myriad of tasks ahead of him), then staggered in to face whatever lay before me.

By now a peace had come over me, and I just knew I could trust God to take care of me. I thought of Mary and how she had had to travel before the birth of Jesus. What rough roads she journeyed over before reaching an inn that had no room! There were no kind nurses waiting for her, only a stable that was to be her maternity room. Her faith inspired me, as I realized how fortunate I was to have a doctor who was genuinely concerned for his patient. Dr. Dorrough stayed with me all day and was always by my side when the going started to get rough. In between whiffs of twilight sleep ("Your Queen used this at the birth of her children."), he would whisper words of encouragement. I learned afterwards that he had cancelled all appointments for that day. He knew of my mother's death and said, "You were away from your family, and I wanted to do everything I could to help at this time." The Lord had surely touched the heart of this overwhelmingly busy doctor so that I could be comforted instead of fearful.

Billy, Jr., was finally born at nine-thirty in the evening; he weighed a bit over ten pounds. He had an expression on his face that seemed to say, "All right, world, I finally made it!" He did not look like a newborn baby but appeared to be at least a month old, which the doctor was sure he was!

As I held him in my arms, with Bill standing beside me, I felt it was a miracle. I find it hard to understand how any woman cannot believe in God when she looks for the first time into the face of the new creation she has been carrying within her for nine months. I found it awesome as I watched little Bill sleeping contentedly, oblivious of the joy his arrival had given us.

Bill had a small card printed to include in each birth announcement. It read:

My Son

I saw you for the first time today. The nurse held you up so that I could get a good look at you through the nursery window. I felt very proud. You were my son!

I was proud and thankful too—thankful to God for you, thankful that you were well and strong, with your tiny body in proper working order. Your mother and I had prayed that it might be so. And seeing you as you were today was the answer to our prayers.

And there were other things we had prayed about, things we shall continue to pray about as you grow up. That our words and our lives may lead you to know the Saviour that we know. That you may not only belong to us, but to Him. For we know of nothing better than a life in Christ, and we wish the best for you.

Arriving home from the hospital, I learned we would be moving in three weeks. Bill had been asked to go to New York to help set up the scheduled Crusade that Billy Graham would be holding in Madison Square Garden.

We packed to move to New York, and I felt mad at the world. I was so tired! Here I was having to move out of this house with a newborn baby. "Well, Lord, please don't ever let this happen again. If I ever have another child, I want to be settled and have time to enjoy him—not this confounded packing."

On our way to New York, we stopped at Montreat to see Billy and Ruth Graham. We stayed with Ruth's parents, Dr. and Mrs. Bell, two of the dearest Christians I have ever met. It was in their home, before I was married, that I had spent my first American Thanksgiving. I shall never forget the warmth of their friendliness, the glow of their home, and the tremendous feeling of thanksgiving that came over me as I sat at the table with their family to celebrate a holiday that was completely foreign to me.

Now I was in their home once more, a wife and a mother. A *mother*. I still was not used to that word applying to me. Before we left Montgomery, Alabama, I had to call City Hall to ask them to send my son's birth certificate. *My son* made me glow as I thought of the full meaning of it all.

One evening we went up the mountain to the Grahams' house and asked Billy to dedicate Bill, Jr., to the Lord. For this Anglican it was a real compromise. I had always secretly hoped he would be dressed in a beautiful white robe and be christened in a church which had stained-glass windows. My family and Bill's would be there. But it was a beautiful service in their living room and holds a very special place in our hearts. After Billy dedicated him to the Lord, Ruth looked at the sleeping baby and said, "Why, look— he's dead to the world."

We stayed a year in New York. I began to experience the tremendous adjustment mothers go through when suddenly confined to being home with a baby. The frustration was mixed with guilt because I missed being able to go out when I wanted to. But there were so many happy times in New York with Bill, Jr., watching him grow, responding to love, seeing him smile. We lived in a section that did not have a park, and the only "safe" area for walking was around the block of the apartment building. It was sad to see so many derelicts and winos on the street. Often, I would have to push the stroller around where they lay on the pavement sleeping off the effects of the alcohol.

One day in a drugstore, one staggered over to me and said, "What a beautiful baby you have." Then he burst out crying. Bending down to Bill, Jr., he said to him, "Never become like me, son. I'm a wino and I've wasted my life." It was heartbreaking to see this shell of a man. I stood and talked with him for a while, telling him that his life was not hopeless, that God loved him no matter what had happened before in his life. He grabbed my hands and thanked me and then was gone into the maze of humanity once more. I often wonder what became of him and whether he ever really asked the Lord to come into his life and help him. Standing there I could not judge that scarred human being. What circumstances had brought him to the excruciating loneliness that must have been his constant companion? Only the cheap alcohol that blotted out the agonizing memories was his gruesome comrade. It was gradually destroying this man who once had been a little boy like mine.

Bill's work next took us to Australia. Little Bill loved the koala bears, kangaroos, and the kookaburra that lived in a tree outside his bedroom window. Each morning he would be awakened by the laughing sound of this delightful bird.

The Crusade was a tremendous success. The dedicated spirit of the Australian Christians pervaded everything they set out to do.

I shall never forget the communion service Bill and I attended one Sunday at Donald Begbie's church in a suburb of Sydney. Never have I heard the words of the Anglican Communion service spoken with more feeling. When I took the bread and the wine, I was brought to a deepening consciousness of the sacrifice of our Lord. "This is my body, broken for *you*...." So often I had taken this service for granted, but again I was reminded of all it really means. Jesus' willingness to die on that cross, paying such a price, makes communion the most costly meal in history. It was an act of love that would surpass anything else that could possibly come into my life. To see so many thousands of people giving their lives to this Saviour at the Sydney Crusade was an intensely moving sight.

When our days in Australia were over, we said a regretful goodbye to so many people who had become close friends. We began our long trip back home, via England. Now I was expecting another baby, but I was not to be deterred from visiting as many countries as possible on our way back.

It was an incredible trip. We stopped over in New Guinea, Manila, and then Hong Kong. I was saddened by the sight of so much poverty next door to the luxurious hotels.

As we boarded the plane leaving Hong Kong for India, I remember thinking, "Good, it has Rolls Royce engines—we'll be safe with them."

Half an hour outside of Calcutta, we ran into a very bad thunderstorm and had to keep circling. I looked out but could see nothing but rain beating on the windows. Stewardesses were now running up and down the aisles, looking rather panicky, and taking down any luggage that had been left overhead.

We made our descent, swerving in the high winds. Suddenly there was a loud crash, and—with a tremendous lurch—the plane ascended once more!

Bill, Jr., said very calmly, "I think the big bad wolf is going to make this plane crash!" Wonderful words when you are in a blinding storm!

If this is true, I thought, *my life should start to appear before my eyes.* But nothing happened, in fact my mind went completely blank. At first I could not even remember a verse of Scripture. Then the verse in Psalm 37 came to my mind, the one that Miss Henrietta Mears had prayed with me in Hollywood: "Commit thy

way unto the Lord; trust also in him; and he shall bring it to pass"
(v. 5).

I kept repeating it over and over again. I did commit us all to
Him and just prayed He would bring this aircraft down safely. The
pilot started another approach for landing and we all held on,
white-knuckled and breathing heavily. Again there was a huge
crash, and we bumped onto the landing strip with a jolt. What a
relief; we were down! Bill undid his seat belt and relaxed. Still holding onto Bill, Jr., I was wide-eyed, but so thankful to be on terra
firma. Suddenly the terra was not so firma as we began to bump
and get shot all over the plane. The brakes had failed, and the plane
was taking off across a soggy rice-paddy. Luckily we finally came
to a halt.

The pilot rushed out of his cabin and brushed past us to look out
of the window at the engines, making sure they were not going to
catch fire. The men were told to get off first. "I always thought it
was women and children first," I said to Bill, Jr., as I busily put on
our raincoats. A calm had descended over me that was not of my
own making, for I had committed our way to the Lord, and again
He had taken care of us.

The men were needed to hoist out the canvas chute. We were all
pushed down it to the safety of the muddy field. I wondered about
snakes, but tried to think of something else. Fifteen minutes later
the ambulances, crash wagons, and fire engines arrived. It was a
comforting sight! We were boarded onto a bus and taken to the
main terminal of Dum-Dum airport. I thought that was a good
name for it. After the fright of it was over, it was funny to see our
fellow passengers traipsing around with mud stains over their
ankles. You could easily tell who had been on the ill-fated flight.

We were told that one wing had hit something on the first attempt to land, and the other wing had hit a tree as we landed. What
saved us were the Rolls Royce engines that were strong enough to
send the plane up the second time.

"Thank you, Rolls Royce, and thank You, Lord."

We were taken to a hotel for the night. Perhaps the drive in the
taxi to get there was more frightening than the crash. The doors

were done up with string, and the driver never seemed to look where he was going as he swerved amidst people walking in the streets. The only time he seemed to be really conscious of his surroundings was when he had to slow down to avoid a sacred cow.

I could not believe the sight of those people! I looked out of the taxi window and saw so many men and young boys preparing to sleep on the streets. Each day many die and are carted away, making space for more hungry, desolate souls.

When we left Australia we had not intended to stay overnight in India. Because of its heat, we felt it better for me to stop in a cooler country. I am glad we had to stop there, for the experience made India more than a statistic to me. It would be hard to forget the heartache, hunger, and the humiliation of the masses who had to forage for food daily in order to exist. It would not be enough for me to walk through the streets saying to them, "Jesus loves you," when all around was stench and poverty such as I had never seen before. To reach these dear souls for Christ would take acts of mercy such as He had shown. It would take the devotion of someone like Sister Teresa who has dedicated her life to them and opened a home for the dying. Amid all the heartache, she goes on giving hope and love to so many.

As we left Calcutta the next day, I looked out of our plane window and saw the wreck of our ill-fated Comet. It was sitting there like a wounded bird, its wings broken. Abruptly my thoughts turned to the child I was carrying within me. I had taken for granted we were all safe yesterday, but would there be damage to this little growing soul? The impact had been jarring to my whole body—could it precipitate a miscarriage? I began to pray again that everything would be all right.

16

In Indianapolis I enrolled in natural childbirth classes, having read so much about the method. After Bill, Jr.,'s birth I had felt cheated, somehow. This time I wanted to be conscious, so that I could welcome my second baby into the world.

I looked around at all the fellow walruses puffing and blowing while we exercised and laughed. I learned that our instructor, Carol Bonham, was a Christian who was taking counseling classes for the Billy Graham Crusade. A friendship was established; here once again God had reached down and said, "You are not without friends in a strange city, because there are those who love Me here...."

One Sunday evening, while we were watching "Lassie" on TV (it being Bill, Jr.,'s favorite program), I suddenly began to have pains. I thought it was something I had eaten, but the pains became worse, and I staggered into the bathroom. Three-year-old Bill, Jr., came in after me and wanted to know what was wrong.

"Not feeling too good, Mother? 'Dennis the Menace' is coming on next, Mom, and that will make you feel better!"

I realized my own little "Dennis" was on the way and I yelled out to Bill to get the car. He telephoned a friend to come to stay with Bill, Jr. It was snowing, and I was sure we would never make it to the hospital in time. We sped down the road, slipping and sliding, praying and praying.

At the hospital I kissed Bill goodbye and was whisked in a wheel-chair into an elevator. Then began the countdown. Less than half an hour later I was wheeled into the delivery room. While I was try-ing to remember all my exercises for relaxing, the anesthetist asked if I wanted a nice whiff to set me off to sleep! I told him I didn't, for the Lord had assured me it was going to be all right.

In a mirror I saw my second son being born; it was a moment that I shared with the Lord. I cried out to Him my thankfulness and praise that He had again entrusted me with one of His creations. There was pain; but it was bearable. I knew that as I worked with the doctor the miracle of birth was being enacted and I was part of the incredible production that was God's. I held my little son in my arms as they wheeled me out of the delivery room.

The young intern who had been present came and asked if he could talk with me for a while. He sat by my bed and said, "I've seen many births now and I have heard women scream and curse God for the pain, but you were thanking Him. I wonder if birth shouldn't always be like that?"

I was able to tell him that Jesus was so close to me in that delivery room, and that it was the most natural thing in the world for me to want to thank Him for my little son. Then too, I was able to tell him that basically I am a coward—terrified of anything to do with a hospital or pain. But it was His grace that took my fears away and made the birth of my child a beautiful and glorious experience. The promise is, "He shall gently lead those that are with young" (*see* Isaiah 40:11). He had gently led me over many thousands of miles, calmed all my fears, and had given me two sons to bring us joy.

We called the baby David after the Psalmist, and I prayed the same prayer that I did when Bill, Jr., was born:

> Lord, this child is a gift from You. Help me to love him,
> care for him, teach him of Your great love, and then when
> the time comes to let him go out in the world, give me
> Your grace and strength not to hold on to him.

This prayer proves harder as the years go by. "To let him go...." Our sons have become so much a part of our lives, it would be very easy for me to play the role of the possessive mother. But Bill and I realize we are merely custodians of their lives here on earth until they reach the age when they must stand alone.

Above all I have tried to teach them that they will *never be alone.*

No matter what the situation, Christ who has come into their lives, will *always* be there. *Always*. What a wonderful word that is when applied to His love.

Remember what I had told the Lord about being settled the next time I had a baby? Well here I was again in exactly the same predicament, for we were to move to Philadelphia three weeks after David was born.

Trying to pack, still feeling very weak, and with two children to care for, I had an award-winning attack of the blues which besiege most mothers after the birth of a child. The Lord had foreseen my need and had already brought into my life someone who volunteered to help me. Ginny Booth had been working in the Crusade office, and she took over so many tasks for me as I struggled to regain my strength and pack for the journey to Philadelphia. He knew I could never have made it without her. Ginny became Bill's secretary for quite some time, and we all grew to love her as one of our family.

The day of departure dawned, and I went to awaken Bill, Jr., early. I was horrified by what I saw—his face was covered with red spots—measles! Now we would have to leave with a three-week-old baby and a sick child. What a journey to Philadelphia!

We had been in Philadelphia only a few months when a cablegram came from England. Opening it, I read: "Daddy died this morning. Please phone. Love, Ann." I read it over and over to try to comprehend what the words meant. I sat in shock trying to sort out the thoughts that crowded my mind. Daddy was dead, and the indescribable agony of grief swept over me. To think I would not see his face again, nor hear his voice.

Bill, feeling my hurt, put his comforting arms around me. Together we sobbed out our sorrow to Christ, locked in the depths of anguish that grips everyone when they experience the loss of someone dear to them. Through my tears I remembered that the night before as I was reading the Bible, I had been struck by a verse in Revelation:

And I heard a voice from heaven saying unto me, Write,
Blessed are the dead which die in the Lord from henceforth:
Yea, saith the Spirit, that they may rest from their labours; and
their works do follow them.

Revelation 14:13

I had read this over and over, wondering who the Lord might be
bringing to my mind. There was no one I knew at that time who
was ill, and finally I dismissed the thoughts. Now, as I sat shattered
by the news of Daddy's passing, those words came back to comfort
my heart. Daddy was resting now. He had suffered so much over
the years due to his health. His work kept him traveling over England in a car that had no heater. He had often come home frozen
from the long hours spent driving from city to city.

I called Ann. The overseas connection was not very clear, but I
heard her say that Daddy had rushed across the road to aid a neighbor who had been overcome by gas from an unlighted burner. In
rescuing her, he had suffered a fatal heart attack. Ann sounded so
desolate.

That night I sat by the window of our apartment watching the
sunset—watching until the sun finally dropped out of view. I was
thinking of a man who, in the world's estimation, could not be
termed a success. A few weeks earlier he had written me telling of
the disappointment he had received in his work. The owner of the
company had died; now younger men had stepped in, and he was
not to receive the promotion the owner had been promising him. "I
feel such a failure," he wrote. "I have not achieved all I had
hoped."

Daddy's letter moved me deeply. I sat down and wrote immediately, telling him never to think of himself as a failure. We often
evaluate *success* by how much money we have in the bank. How
many men who made fortunes were the kind of husbands or fathers
they should have been? I told him that I was so grateful to the Lord
for a father who always understood and who was always interested
in all my activities. Though I hurt him in so many ways, his love
was unchanging. To me he epitomized success, for he was a man

who never compromised to attain recognition and was ready to help anyone at any time. "No, Daddy, you are not a failure. Please remember this and know how much I love you."

How thankful I was that I had not procrastinated, as is my habit when writing letters, but had sent that letter to him. Sitting there by the window, I felt the Comforter that Christ said He would send. The distance that had separated Daddy and me no longer mattered. My father was with Him and He was not even a breath away.

The next day I collected my mail; there was a letter in my father's familiar hand, written a few days before he died. In it he asked just when he would be able to see his dear grandson, David, and remembered the happy times he had spent with Bill, Jr. He said his thoughts and prayers were with us. His last words, "God bless you all," rang in my ears, as I remembered the voice that had guided me over the years.

Some time later I made a journey to England with the boys. Bill saw us off on his way to South America. The hardest part for me was to arrive at the airport, walk through the waiting lounge, and not see Daddy there to greet us.

One day, months later, I got to thinking of how much I would love to have been able to visit with my father. Now he was dead; I missed his letters so much. They were always encouraging and resounded with his endearing personality. Standing by the sink in the kitchen, I suddenly said to the Lord, "Oh, if only Daddy were alive!" And the heartache of my grief swept over me again.

"But he is! So much more than he has ever been!"

I looked up startled and then realized the Lord had given these thoughts to me. They flooded over me like a soothing balm and their comfort surrounded me.

"Thank You, Lord, of course he is," I said through my tears.

I thought of all the illness he had endured—I could not wish him back. If only he could have met his other grandson, it would have given him such pleasure. David would not know this gentle man who had a delightful sense of humor and a great sense of loyalty to those he loved. But one day David will. What reunions we shall have with those we love in Christ! I often try to imagine our meeting again. Until then I have such wonderful memories.

One particular memory stands out. Shortly after my mother died, Daddy had taken me for a holiday at Selsey in Sussex. We stayed in a little hotel overlooking the bay. From our bedroom window I could see the little boats and sea gulls and imagine all kinds of adventures that lay across the horizon.

A storm was brewing out at sea, and I watched the black clouds rolling closer towards the shore. It began to rain as I got ready for bed. Daddy was downstairs talking to some of the other guests when a huge flash of lightning, followed by a deafening clap of thunder, made the lights go out. Nanny had always told me that thunder was "God getting the coals," but this did not comfort me that night in the darkness of my strange bedroom. I began to cry, frightened, wondering where my father was.

Then I heard his voice calling to me as he came up the stairs, "Don't be afraid, Joan. I'm here. Everything is all right." The sound of his voice reassuring me took away all my fears, and his presence in the bedroom enabled me to sleep peacefully, knowing he would protect me.

When we come to the point of death we will all need a shepherd. Just as Daddy had been my shepherd that night in the darkness, so Christ was his shepherd as he crossed the unknown span that we all will have to face one day.

During the Los Angeles Crusade, Bill and I were invited to Debbie Reynolds's home in Beverly Hills. It was to be an informal get-together around ten o'clock in the evening.

Colleen Townsend Evans, a friend of Debbie's, had helped to arrange it. Debbie invited Billy Graham to meet several of her friends; the guest list included Glenn Ford, Edie Adams, Jack Lemmon and his beautiful wife, Felicia Farr, and Mary Costa, the opera singer. But the name on the list of invited guests that interested me the most was that of Judy Garland.

When we drove up to the impressive house, my thoughts were basically of Judy. I had been praying for her for a long time. She was a sensitive soul, caught in a treadmill that was not altogether of her own making. Her teen years were spent becoming a star tailored to the studio's wishes. Because of the tremendous stresses and strains, the inevitable pep pills were used to get her going on the set. There was the insatiable craving deep within her to be loved and understood. Her attempted suicides haunted me, and I had so often prayed that she would find the same answer I had found to my desperate search for peace.

When we walked into Debbie's den, most of the guests had arrived. But Judy was missing. I was deeply disappointed.

After a time a discussion started, and one of the guests questioned Billy Graham, "What *is* sin?"

Billy expounded at great length, and I watched each face. They were all intent, listening. Then I heard the door open, and Judy Garland stood there.

To see her face was quite a shock to me. Her eyes betrayed the years of agony she had gone through. This great performer had · paid dearly for the joy she had given to so many. She hesitated and then began to walk toward the couch where I was sitting. I moved over, and she sat down next to me. Whispering introductions, we then turned our attention to Billy Graham and listened as he told of God's inestimable love.

Suddenly Billy turned to me and said, "Joan, why don't you tell what has happened in your life?" All faces turned towards me. Judy looked at me and smiled that beautiful smile as if in encouragement.

I began to tell of all my innermost fears and longings, my breakdowns, and then my contemplated suicide. I told how the Lord had come in and given me hope where there had been nothing but despair, and now I was assured of His love in my life. After I finished speaking there was complete silence.

Then I felt a hand on my arm. It was Judy's. "That was beautiful, darling. But you see—you had a need. I don't have any need." Incredulously, I looked into her face, remembering all she had been through, and could hardly believe what I was hearing. Perhaps there was no other person in Hollywood who had such a need as Judy, to be loved, to be needed—not because of what she had achieved, but to be loved and understood for herself.

Maybe the many pills she had taken numbed her into this euphoria, as they had done in my own life. It was only when I was alone, and their effects wore off, that I knew I had to find an answer to the constant gnawing deep within and the agonizing loneliness.

When I read of Judy's death (possibly of an overdose) while she was living in London a few years later I cried as if one of my own family had died. I had walked the same horrendous path and, but for His grace, might have ended my life too. I cannot judge her. When I had taken my phenobarbital tablets, I would sometimes forget if I had had them; it was easy to take a second dose, and then a third, and then....

Judy heard of our Heavenly Father's love that night at Debbie Reynolds's house. I do believe in a God who is ready to receive us, no matter how late. Recently I learned that in the last few years of her life, Judy always carried a Bible with her wherever she traveled. It was the gift of a minister of whom she was very fond. Her favorite chapter was the Love Chapter in Corinthians in which Paul says love goes on forever. (*See* 1 Corinthians 13, LB.)

When I heard the news that Bill was to be sent to London to organize the Earls Court Crusade there, I was overjoyed! To think of being able to live there with him and the boys! I could think of nothing more wonderful, because I could introduce them to so much that I loved in that city. I have had an unashamed love affair with London ever since I can remember. Samuel Johnson had said, "When you are tired of London, you are tired of life." Westminster Abbey, Buckingham Palace, and the Tower of London are not mere tourist spots to me, they are part of my heritage. Sometimes I just get homesick to walk down Piccadilly and take in all the sights and sounds that make up London.

In London we searched for some time to find accommodations that would be suitable for a family of four. We found a little row house in Chelsea, and I fell in love with it instantly. There was not enough room to "swing a cat" once Bill and the boys entered one of the small rooms, but we all agreed we hoped we could rent it. We worked out the financial arrangements with the landlord and were able to move in.

This house welcomed you as soon as you opened the front door. There was a large brass lion's head on the door to greet one. The rooms were decorated with antiques; and the landlord, an interior decorator, had bathed the walls in sunny colors. The combination was beautiful.

The boys had grown to admire and respect antiques, having an antique freak for a mother, so I did not have to worry about their destroying the Regency fretwork tea table in the living room or the exquisite miniatures which hung in the bathroom. This little house had two small rooms on each of its three floors. It had been built in the 1800s to accommodate the families of the servants who worked in the large stately homes in nearby streets.

It was delightful being able to entertain my family so often. Ann and Geraldine (my stepmother and half sister) would come up from Eastbourne. My Aunt Hilda and cousin Audrey would visit us, and then in the evening my Uncle and Audrey's husband, John, would join us for dinner. I felt very much like the settled housewife entertaining family and friends in my old country.

One day, not too long after moving into our little row house, I was reading to David as he lay in bed suffering from the ordeal of measles. We heard the fire engines roar down our little street and come to a grinding halt outside our house. I looked out of the bedroom window and saw that the firemen were racing into the house next door, which had been made into apartments. Smoke was billowing out of the windows, and I decided it was time to prepare for a quick evacuation if necessary. I bundled David up in some blankets and took him downstairs, waiting to see if we would have to leave. I felt the walls of our house. They were getting hot, but the firemen soon put out the blaze, and we were told there was no danger. We were so relieved.

Next day I read in the paper that the fire had happened in an apartment belonging to Sarah Churchill. She was merely staying there while her beautiful Eaton Square residence was being refurbished. I wrote her a note saying how sorry I was to hear about the fire. To keep from appearing to push myself, I added that I did not like nosy neighbors, but knew there were often crises that beset one. I hoped that she would feel free to call on us, if we could be of any help. She sent back a beautiful note thanking me and saying she hoped we would soon meet.

A very warm friendship developed from this, and her surprise knocks on our front door heralded delightful hours spent talking over tea. I had loved her father so much and realized that the children of famous people often sacrifice tremendously, as the world competes for their attention. But she told of the warmth of this man; though having to deal with the heavy burdens of state, he loved to talk with her, and there was a great bond between them.

One night she arrived on our doorstep asking if she could visit with her "angels"—as she called Bill and me. I told her if we were angels, our halos were mighty crooked! Not to be deterred, we talked for hours about the Lord we knew. She said she didn't want to "join," but she loved Him too. I explained that you didn't have to "join" anything, but it was a question of giving yourself to this Christ and asking Him into your life.

Later she asked if she could go in to see the children sleeping in their bunk beds. Tenderly she touched them on their heads. As she bent over them her beautiful long red hair made me think how much she looked like Mary Magdalene. I remembered how much Jesus had loved her and thought how He loves Sarah, who has experienced so much tragedy in her life.

If you have ever read any of her poetry, you will understand so much about this woman. Her ability to express herself is a great gift. To read her poetry is to know her feelings bared. Christ sees this lovely soul, understanding as no human can, all that the heart is capable of bearing alone. And yet not alone—for He is there!

These lines from Sarah's poem titled "Loneliness" describe vividly the torture that many face each day:

> Loneliness
> Is the limit of your eye and feeling
> Loneliness is beyond safe horizons
> Loneliness is where there is no explanation
> No reason ever asked
> Loneliness is the stars
> The falling spaces
> Loneliness is a void on which
> You must force dimensions
> If you are to survive the endless years

I feel such a tremendous affinity for Sarah. She has put into words what this distraught soul also had experienced for so many years.

I often walked in Hyde Park, Kensington Gardens, and St. James's Park remembering how much had happened over the years since I had gone there before. Then I had been searching to find answers to the multitudinous questions that would flood my mind. My life did have meaning now. I had a husband who loved me, and I loved him; we were complete opposites, and yet we both met each other's needs in so many ways. I had to come to grips with the realization that Bill was not perfect, and so did he in regard to me. When we were first married, we had put each other on a pedestal, and how quickly the pedestal cracked! Mine cracked a lot quicker than Bill's—it was made of a very cheap kind of clay! I had heard Archbishop Fulton Sheen once say on television that husbands and wives expected too much from each other. They were only the spark of love, but God was the flame. If we always looked to Him for our complete satisfaction in life, we would never be disappointed with each other. This helped me so much; it was an illustration I have had to keep drawing upon through my marriage, for the human in me has wanted perfection and demanded far too much of anyone.

Continuing to walk, I would think of my other blessings—the

boys. Both were so different in temperament, but both were so dear to me. They were such a handful while we were in London. David was six and Billy nine. It was perpetual motion from morning until night, and the escapades never ceased. David was caught playing truant, having gone to Battersea Fun Fair for the day (complete with friend and cigars). Billy spent every available moment at the London Zoo and seemed to live in an animal world. His ambition, then, was to be a zoo keeper.

One day he decided to run away from home. He carefully packed a small suitcase with his collection of miniature animals and determinedly strode out into the night. Five minutes later he returned, announcing he would wait until after supper. We knew the call of food would be stronger than the call of the wild! After a good meal and some laughs with us, he decided to postpone the venture indefinitely.

But how I loved them. Their trust in me caused me to remember Jesus' words: "Except ye be converted, and become as little children, ye shall not enter into the kingdom of heaven" (*see* Matthew 18:3). They did not question that we loved them, and they simply expected to be fed and clothed. God had surely done that for me.

The times I had questioned God's will in my life! There was a great deal of trial and error before I was convinced that His will was perfect. There would be clashes of will; and even today, I have to go on learning the lesson of being able to say, "Not my will but Thine be done." (Only recently did I find out that apart from Scottish and English blood, my ancestors had bestowed on me Irish blood too. So when the three of them get going it is no wonder I have my troubles! The English part seems to be the one that can face society, cool, calm, and seemingly unruffled; but when the other two meet in the privacy of my home, or in the heat of battles raging in my mind, it's World War II all over again!)

The meetings at Earls Court went extremely well. The double-decker buses advertised: BILLY'S BACK! Everywhere people were talking about the Crusade—pro and con. It all brought back memories of Harringay where I had sat as a spectator, and had gone home as a partaker of His love and compassion.

This time I was counseling those who had come forward, helping them to take their first few steps in the Christian life. I could not tell them they would have no more problems, for I had not experienced this, and God had not promised it either. But I was able to tell them that over the years it had been His strength that had kept me. There are still times when I have completely messed up and failed those I love and the Lord, too. But He forgives and helps me over my frailties.

Oliver Goldsmith, the English playwright, said, "Our greatest glory consists not in never falling, but in rising every time we fall." Many times it would be impossible for me to rise without the Lord. It reminds me of when the boys were learning to walk. They would do so well for a couple of steps and then crash—down they would go! Looking up to me or Bill, they would seek our help to stand them up again. Then they would go precariously on their way, learning to balance, so that they could one day walk securely.

For me, the memorable night of the London Crusade was the night when my stepmother, Ann, and my sister, Geraldine, walked forward to give their lives to Christ. They had experienced such loneliness since the death of my father, and I had prayed so much that they would come to know the full extent of His love. "But my God shall supply all your need according to his riches in glory by Christ Jesus" (Philippians 4:19).

At Earls Court I counseled many girls who felt their lives could never be changed; the same hopelessness that pervaded their thoughts had been the tenant of my mind.

At the Crusade I was introduced to Rose (I have changed her name) while she was still under the influence of drugs. She was a frantic young girl of seventeen. Her dark hair was as wild as her eyes and she needed help so desperately. The night before, alone and in a drugged state, she had hallucinated. She screamed out, for she saw and felt black spiders crawling all over her. I learned she had run away from home and was actively selling drugs in London at the age of fourteen. There was not too much of life that Rose had not experienced. Gradually I was able to win her confidence, and I saw her begin to trust Jesus to help her.

I would meet her in Hyde Park. Sitting by the Serpentine, watching the boats and the crowds who had come to relax in the sun, she would proceed to empty her handbag of its contents of drugs and say, in her Cockney voice, " 'Ere, Joan, you take 'em and get rid of 'em. I'm really trying to quit—honest I am.''

I would take whatever she gave me and flush them down the toilet. One day, however, I decided to keep a packet and take it to a meeting where I was to speak the next day. It would make a good illustration for me as I talked about the drugs that were destroying the minds of the young people. As an afterthought, I decided to get rid of the drug in the usual way and keep the silver foil it was wrapped in. I was so green! I could easily have been stopped and arrested for possession of drugs. (That next week a minister *was* arrested after showing his congregation a small package of marijuana.)

But I was also so green in my handling of Rose! She had told me she was on marijuana and hashish, and here she had been giving me heroin! It was only when she gave me a hypodermic needle to get rid of that I began to realize what was happening. Her brother had been hooked on heroin for some time.

Rose was completely uninhibited, especially when she was coming off a high. Once when we were walking in St. James's Park, she suddenly threw her dress up over her head and began scratching. She complained, "Oooh, these mosquitoes are killing me!" The men in bowler hats, who passed us at the time, merely raised their eyebrows and proceeded along the path as if nothing had happened.

Sometimes, in the middle of the night, she would call for help. Bill would go to get her; he'd find her crumpled in a telephone booth, out cold. She finally went to live with a family in the country who had a large house, and even larger hearts. Here Rose began to feel she was wanted and understood. As time went on, she was able to quit the drugs and would come up to London to see us. Her eyes were no longer foggy from drug use, and she was bright and happy. The scars were still there, and always would be, but Jesus had helped this girl who had been on the verge of destroying herself.

Rose had many problems—many highs and lows, and it was not

an easy walk for her. She went on to help her brother and others find a way out of the destructive maze they were in.

During our stay in London, Bill and I visited my grandmother as often as we could. She was in a hospital and had been ill for some time. It was heartbreaking to see her lying there with seemingly no purpose for living, and no reassurance of a life to come. Each time we would end our visit holding her hands and praying. There would always be the same reaction—a blank stare from Nanny, and no comment whatsoever. I thought of what she had said to me when I had explained how Christ had come into my life and brought hope and His love.

"It's too late for me," she had said, "I'm too old to change."

On our way out, passing the other white, sterile rooms with their elderly occupants, I would wonder: Does she resent our prayers? Would it be better not to pray with her? *Oh, Lord, please don't let her die without knowing You!*

One day I was in our bedroom, in the little house in Chelsea, making the bed. It seemed the Lord said to me, "Today is the day. Ask Nanny again about Me!"

Quickly my mind raced—ask Bill to say something to her—perhaps I'm too close to her. She knows too much about me as a child. She'll remember all my faults. Perhaps that is what has stopped her from believing.

In the car on the way to the hospital, I confided my thoughts to Bill, glad to rid myself of any responsibility.

"No," he said, "*you* ask her. The Lord told you, not me, to do it."

I looked out of the corner of my eye, saw the set of his chin, and knew—that was that.

Bill even waited outside the hospital in the car, so it meant I was completely alone. Only, not really. The Lord felt very close to me as I started to walk down the long corridors to Nanny's room.

Reaching it, I was told Nanny had worsened. Walking into her private room, I saw her lying there, small and helpless, in the stark hospital bed. The room was devoid of any decoration, and this made her seem even more the poignant focus of attention.

"Nanny," I whispered. She opened her eyes, and there was a slight flicker of recognition. I took her hand.

I remembered, as I looked at that work-worn hand, how many times it had helped me over many heartaches. How many times I had held it as we had gone on so many adventures together during my childhood. I desperately wanted to convey to her my thanks and love for all she had ever done for me. Now the nurse had said it may not be long before the end.

"Dear Lord," I silently prayed, "please give me the right words to say."

Involuntarily it seemed, I began to whisper to her, "Nanny, do you know that Jesus loves you?"

"Yes," she said very softly.

"And do you know He has a place waiting for you that is far more beautiful than anything you have ever seen?"

I told her there is a verse in the Bible that says, "For since the beginning of the world men have not heard, nor perceived by the ear, neither hath the eye seen, O God, beside thee, what he hath prepared for him that waiteth for him" (Isaiah 64:4).

Her whole face lit up as she said, "Yes, I know!"

Her limp hand, which I was still holding, pressed mine in silent affirmation. I looked at her face, and Nanny never looked more beautiful to me, for now there was an expression of joy and hope in her eyes.

I leaned over and kissed her and told her how much I loved her, and that one day we would all be together again. She smiled and nodded.

As I called, "Goodbye," at the door of her room, she waved to me, and her face relayed the peace she had now found. That is my last memory of her.

She died a few hours later. The nurse told us that after I had left, Nanny said to her, "I'm not afraid to die any more," and then slipped into a coma from which she never awakened.

How thankful I was to the Lord that Nanny was with Him, suffering no more pain, and in a place that *was* far more beautiful than she had ever known.

The tears I shed were human ones, as there was the natural grief of losing a loved one; but they were also tears of gratitude that she was with Christ, and that we are never too old to find Him if we really want to.

18

Towards the end of our stay in London, the days were marred by Bill's sudden hemorrhaging. I tried several times to get him to see a doctor, but he insisted on waiting until we returned to the States in a month or so. Confiding in my London doctor, my fears grew, as she told me just what to expect. The hemorrhaging stopped, but there were always the nagging fears in the back of my mind.

We settled into a rented house outside of New York City upon our return to the States. It was unfurnished, so we went to scores of garage sales and bought the furniture piece by piece—hauling it ourselves. Even the Chinese Chippendale bedroom set that weighed a ton!

The neighbors got used to seeing the Browns arrive with an unexpected "treasure" and hearing us shout as we heaved the objects up the front steps. I would have to rest every few feet, and a frustrated "moving man" would be yelling, "Now what's the matter? *Heave!*"

In a year we would have to dismantle everything and head on for fields unknown. Even though it was so temporary, we tried to give the boys a feeling of security.

Bill established an office in New York and departed each day on the train. The boys were going to the local school and made friends once more. I was feeling very homesick for London with its instant transportation. "I'm not a suburban person, Lord, so why do I get stuck out here? It's all right for Bill. He goes into a city, establishes his office, and presto, he's running again. The boys go to their school, and life seems to be the same for them. But here am I, stuck in the house, when I could be out *doing* all kinds of things!" I bemoaned my fate as a suburban housewife, caught in the machinery of supermarkets, laundry, dust, and cooking. The Lord had heard me talk like this before in other locations, so it was nothing new. Well, that was my lot, and with self-pity I gritted my teeth and acted out the part of the contented housewife—which I was not.

One morning something happened that made all my bemoanings fade into the background. I heard a cry from our room and, running up the stairs, I saw Bill, his face white and drawn. He had had a tremendous hemorrhage—far worse than before. Immediately I called a friend who recommended a doctor, and Bill and I drove over as fast as we could. He was X-rayed, and then there was the interminable waiting for the result.

The phone rang while I was making the bed the next morning. The doctor's nurse told me Bill would have to call the office as soon as possible. Hesitatingly, I asked her if she could tell me anything.

After a pause she said, "There are lesions."

"Does that mean...?" I hesitated forming the word *cancer*.

"It could," she said.

My hands were wet with sweat. I thanked her and hung up. The house seemed so empty—my whole world was crashing in on me as the sickening feeling of panic engulfed me—me, who "died" inside every time Bill had to go on a trip. Now I was faced with the possibility of his having a major operation and perhaps....

But I must not think of that—I had to keep control.

"Oh God, if only I could spare him all this!"

Just like the many times I had wanted to spare the children from hurts in their lives, I wanted to say, "No, there's been a mistake. These things happen to other people—not us."

I phoned Bill at his office and had to break the news to him. The silence, as he let the news sink in, made me want to cry out to him all of my fears, but I asked the Lord for words of comfort. I found myself blurting out that it was going to be all right. God was going to take care of him.

How He *did* take care of us! On the very day Bill had to enter the hospital, Dorothy Williams arrived from England to stay in our home. She had been a medical missionary in Ghana for many years, and we had arranged for her to come over from England long before we knew of Bill's illness.

Before, when Bill had gone on trips, my heart would always ache as I packed for him. This time it seemed that every emotion I had been holding back would break into a torrent. There was so much I wanted to say to him—how much I loved him—how frightened I was. But I kept these feelings to myself as I asked the Lord for His restraint.

The time came for him to leave. We all went into the living room for prayer together. I do not know whose hand was shaking the most as we all reached out for one another and prayed. The boys, not fully aware of all the implications, asked Jesus to take care of Dad and, with complete faith that He would, kissed him goodbye.

Bill and I drove to the station where he was to get the train into New York City. We had agreed I would go in early the next morning to be with him before the operation. We sat and waited together on the platform. I heard the train coming in the distance and hoped it would break down, but the roar increased as it belted down the track. As it screeched to a halt, I longed to be able to cry out, "Don't go!" I wondered if the driver knew just what his train's assignment was that night.

"See you in the morning," I said, kissing him goodbye.

As I drove away I remembered that was a line from the movie *A Man Called Peter*. When Peter Marshall was being taken to the hospital, those were the last words he said to his wife, Catherine. When Bill and I were first married, we had seen the film and we could not speak for some time afterwards, as we had been so moved by this true story.

On the way home the tears came tumbling down my face. I was simply remembering all the happy times we had had together. Arriving home, I managed to get to my room and shut the door. The floodgates broke, and all my fears and longings were poured out to Christ. I could no longer hide my emotions.

I had to be strong; yet I was so weak. I had two boys who were depending on me. Bill was depending on me too, and all I wanted to do was run—run from this awful nightmare. I didn't even know how to pray, since my agony seemed to envelop me. Reaching for my Bible, I asked God to comfort me and give me His strength. I had none of my own!

Turning to Romans, chapter eight, my eyes fell on the twenty-sixth verse:

Likewise the Spirit also helpeth our infirmities: for we know not what we should pray for as we ought: but the Spirit itself maketh intercession for us with groanings which cannot be uttered.

In my despair it seemed God was showing me I did not have to be eloquent about my need. The groan that comes deep from the heart is understood by Him. There were many groans that night as I poured it all out, unashamedly. As the tears subsided, I began to read in Matthew, chapter nine, where many of Jesus' healings are described. I came to the thirty-fifth verse:

And Jesus went about all the cities and villages, teaching in their synagogues, and preaching the gospel of the kingdom, and healing every sickness and every disease among the people.

It was the words *every sickness and every disease* that calmed me and gave me an inner peace. Suddenly I felt His presence in such a strong way, as if His arms were encircling me and strengthening me. Instantly I knew the Lord had given me this assurance, and I believed from then on that Bill was going to be all right.

Bill called me from the hospital around nine o'clock, and we prayed together. I felt so much stronger and now was able to tell him that the Lord had given me complete confidence about the outcome.

Next morning I awakened early and took the train into New York to be with Bill. As I approached the elevator to go to Bill's room, a sudden feeling of loneliness came over me.

"Oh Lord...if only someone from my family could be with me...."

But again I sensed that *I was not alone.*

The doors of the elevator opened, and I looked into the face of a dear friend—Helen Stewart. She was the nurse who had recommended Bill's doctor, and she was caring for a patient on another floor. During a break she had come up to see Bill and me. I knew the Lord sent her at such a time.

Bill looked so big and helpless lying in his hospital bed, but he was calm while we talked and prayed together.

The footsteps we heard coming down the hall reminded us it was time for his operation. Again the fears hit me, and I asked the Lord to calm me. Bill received a shot, and with a quick *au revoir* he was gone. They had wheeled him out; there, where he had left them, were his slippers—like two small islands— waiting.

I was alone. I felt very tired and curled up in the arm chair. All the sounds of the hospital and the city outside seemed magnified— along with the tense beating of my heart.

A nurse put her head around the door and asked if I would like a cup of tea. Within minutes she was back handing me the much appreciated tea. She told me to let her know if there was anything else she could do. I thought of the words of Jesus, "And if, as my representatives, you give even a cup of cold water to a little child, you will surely be rewarded" (Matthew 10:42,LB). I felt very much like a small frightened child sitting there in that empty room. A simple act of giving me a cup of tea had reassured me again that He was with me. I don't remember the name of that nurse, but I will always remember and be grateful for her kindness.

Sitting there in that impersonal hospital room memories flooded over me—memories of our meeting, our marriage, and the happy years we shared.

After two hours the doctor came to the room to tell me that Bill had come through the operation with flying colors. I was so thankful to him and to the Lord.

"But," he said, "I am still not sure if I was able to remove all of the tumor. It was the largest I have ever operated on."

My heart sank, but I found myself saying, "It's going to be all right. I know the Lord will heal him."

The doctor gave me a long look and then continued, "We will know more in two days when we get the results from the lab. There may be wild cells." Again I felt that dread go through me; but God had promised, and I had to believe everything would be all right.

Bill finally came back to the room, very woozy, but able to smile and say everything was fine. I sat holding his hand for as long as I could. Then it was time for visitors to leave. I stayed in New York that night with Helen Stewart, exhausted and relieved that the operation was over.

The next day was spent with Bill as he made a remarkable recovery. It was all the nurses and I could do to keep him in bed. However in the back of our minds was the result from the lab. Would it be a "pardon" or a sentence of death? God had promised a "pardon." My faith wavered at times, but only for moments, for He had given me that incredible experience with Him at the house that night I had cried out to Him. I had to believe!

Before I left Bill that night, we again prayed together, remembering the result would be known the next day. There was not too much we could express openly, but we felt the comfort of Christ once more.

I had arranged to take the hospital limousine, because it would be very late when I finally arrived home. There were six other passengers in it, so I squeezed in between two ladies on the back seat. It was good to be able to relax and organize my thoughts before reaching home.

"Who is in that hospital?" The strident voice was that of an elderly lady sitting to my left.

"My husband."

"He's going to die!" she said.

Shocked, I turned and looked at her. I saw the face of an old crone, who would have been perfect typecast as a witch in *Macbeth*.

"He's not going to die," I heard myself say. "The Lord has

promised that he is going to be completely healed."

"No," she cackled, "he is going to die. Prepare yourself. Do you have children?"

I nodded.

"Prepare them tonight. Tell them their father is going to die!"

The lady sitting on my right asked her to be quiet, saying I did not need this kind of talk, but on she went getting louder and louder with her grim predictions. I sensed a terrible demonic presence in this woman. Remembering Jesus' name was my defense, I kept talking of Him and His love and promises to me. It was as if I were listening to someone else as my voice kept repeating these assurances.

Finally, after what seemed hours to me, but really had been about forty-five minutes, the car reached my house. I stumbled out the door with the old lady yelling after me, "Don't forget—prepare your children. He's going to die!"

I shall never forget the feeling that swept over my whole body—like I had been punched all over. I managed to run up the front steps. Fumbling with my keys, I finally opened the door, and the security of our "Garage Sale Decor" home embraced me.

The boys were still up, waiting with Dorothy to hear all the news. Somehow I managed to talk to them coherently, and then with a goodnight kiss and hug, they went to bed. A tremendous feeling of love for them swept over me. What a gift they were! At that moment I thanked the Lord again for the love that Bill and I had together, which was now living on in them. I said goodnight and hastily ran up to the bedroom.

Within the privacy of our room, I put my head in the pillow and sobbed out to the Lord all the frightening experience of the woman in the car. I lay there thinking of the fact that God's love did surround me and nothing could harm me. Finally exhausted, I fell into a fitful sleep, remembering what I had to face the next day.

When I got back to the hospital Bill looked drawn and tired; he told me what a terrible time he had had after I left—how he had wrestled with such negative thoughts. His sister Madelaine had died of cancer at the age of thirty-three. That haunted him. But then he opened his Bible to Proverbs 3:1,2: "My son, forget not my law; but let thine heart keep my commandments; for length of days, and long life, and peace, shall they add to thee."

So often Christians dislike the Bible being used as an "instant survival kit," but so often for the Browns a verse has been given just at the right time.

Looking back, I can see how Satan used the old woman and Bill's frightening experience to try to make us doubt.

Finally the doctor arrived and told us the results of the tests. It seemed Bill would improve, but he would have to keep in close touch with the doctor for a while to make certain everything was healing properly. Bill could leave the hospital in a few days. We were both delighted and thanked this quiet, dignified man.

The doctor met me in the hall a few minutes later and said, "Bill may have to come in again. There are some wild cells and I am concerned that they may flare up." Once more I reiterated my belief that everything was going to be all right and thanked him for all he had done.

A few days later Bill came home. What a patient! He was like a big, old walrus squirming around organizing the New York Crusade from the confines of his bed. Here he was, on the phone, twisting and turning, calling out instructions. But, oh, how good it was to have him home once more! I kept looking at him and thanking the Lord for sparing our dear one.

The next day I went to the supermarket to get some groceries. Upon my return, a scene greeted my eyes that I could hardly believe. Bill was mowing the lawn! I jumped out and demanded that he stop at once. "But, honey, the grass really has grown so much...." I ordered him back to bed and without any hesitation called the doctor's office and "snitched" on him. The nurse was horrified and immediately told the doctor, who prescribed some sedation for him. Sedation does not work on Bill. Instead of helping to quiet him down, it seems to have the reverse effect. When he decided to go into the office a week later, just for a few hours, I did not argue. The peace was fantastic!

The time came quickly for Bill's first checkup. As we got ready to go into New York, thoughts again began to whirl around my brain. The old fears began to come back. "Wild cells," the doctor had said, and this haunted me. We were a little late arriving for the appointment, so Bill asked me to go on up to the doctor's office while he found a parking space.

I opened the door and sat down in the waiting room. Picking up a magazine that to me had no words or photographs, I idly turned the pages with my thoughts only on Bill. The doctor came out and seeing me said, "I'm glad you are here. I just want to warn you that Bill will probably have to go back into the hospital."

I shook my head, but did not say anything.

Bill arrived and went in for the examination. I started to shake uncontrollably with a fear that swept over me and refused to diminish. Like a small child I wanted to find something to hold on to, and I reached inside my handbag and saw my small, red Testament. I pulled it out and began to read it. Again, as if the Lord knew how much I needed His comfort, the first verse I read was "...this man doeth many miracles" (John 11:47). I whispered a silent, *Thank You,* and clung to that promise. Nothing had changed at all, just because Bill had to come and have a checkup.

After a while, the door leading into the doctor's office opened, and he came out to speak to me. "I've never seen a healing like this one. There isn't even a trace!"

I was so overwhelmed with joy I wanted to hug this doctor, but the English in me decided it was not the proper thing to do at that moment. Bill came out with a grin from ear to ear. Thanking the doctor we raced out to the elevator and decided to eat at our favorite Chinese restaurant to celebrate.

It has been over seven years now, and each time Bill has gone back for a checkup he has thus far had a clean bill of health. We still get panicky around examination time. Bill especially has all kinds of thoughts swirling round. Once on his way to the doctor's for his yearly checkup, he got a ticket for speeding; his thoughts were miles away!

We are among the fortunate ones who have experienced this. There are others who have found that the Lord has not answered their prayers in this same way. If only there were a pat answer at times like these, but there isn't, and not until we are face-to-face with Christ will we be able to understand why some are healed and others are not. So often it is said, "God makes no mistakes," but to the bereaved that thought is superficial and of little comfort in the midst of the agony they have to bear.

He doesn't make mistakes, even though I have often questioned in my own life why He chooses to take those who often have much to give this world. My little cousin Stewart, who died of leukemia, had a love of life and such a happy future ahead of him. Was it a mistake that God took him even before he had celebrated his sixth birthday? I believe, if we could understand all there is waiting for us when we die, we would confidently say, "No mistake."

Something seemed to be happening in our lives in the months that lay ahead. There would be a questioning as to whether the Lord wanted us to go on indefinitely, moving from city to city. The decision to conduct a Crusade in New York's Shea Stadium the year after Madison Square Garden meant we would have to move again (even within the same city). Our lease was up, and we had actually helped find the new tenants for our house. Then we were told we would be staying on. Our landlords found us a one-bedroom apartment in Bronxville. With the boys in the only bedroom (which became a den and dining room during the day), Bill and I shared the intended dining room as a bedroom. It measured nine feet by twelve feet and was a tight fit!

Bill told me he felt he was coming to the end of organizing Crusades. I was really amazed, as I had thought it would always be his life's work—he loved it! God had given him the gift of being able to organize masses of people, and they responded eagerly to his leadership. Each time we had been required to move I had told the Lord that it was the last time. I just could not face the hassle of traveling any longer with a family.

But each time He would lovingly forgive the outbursts and give me *His* grace to go on. We had prayed so often about whether I should settle down with the boys somewhere, and Bill continue to travel. That would have meant months and months of separation each year. We always felt the moving would be easier than the separation. So, even though I grumbled to the Lord, I thanked Him, too, that we could be together as much as possible.

Bill, Jr., was now entering high school, and these years would be so important to him. In his fifteen years, he had had twenty-one different homes and attended nine different schools. He was gifted with being able to adapt quickly to new surroundings and situations. But for David, it was different. Moving meant leaving friends and familiar surroundings, and it was hard on him. Once we arrived in a new city, however, he made friends quickly, but there was always the difficulty of adjusting to school.

Bill wrote a letter to Billy Graham telling him he felt he wanted to settle down, which would probably mean having to leave the organization. Many years before, when we were temporarily settled in Washington, D.C., he had written a similar letter. Bill had been offered another position and, seeing me so exhausted, he had decided to write to say he would be leaving. As soon as it was mailed, we realized it was written on emotion—not with the leading of the Lord. Imagine our surprise when our letter was returned by Billy's secretary, unopened. Her note with it said Dr. Graham was out of the country for several weeks; since it was marked "Personal," she felt we would want to keep it until he got back. We thanked the Lord and tore up the letter.

This time however, we felt God was leading us to make a change.

Bill had to go to Plymouth, Massachusetts, to do the advance work for the 200th Anniversary Celebration at which Billy Graham would be speaking. I went up from New York with him once or twice, since this was my favorite part of the country. I felt so close to my English heritage; and as a lover of history, I took in all the historical sites. We started looking for a house in Plymouth, and Bill had offers of work in Boston.

However, one day I was back in our little apartment in Bronxville and received a phone call. A familiar voice said, "Hello, Joan, this is Billy Graham." I knew he must have received the letter by now, and I groaned inwardly. Bill was up in Plymouth and here was I, left to face the Chief! I stuttered and stammered—shades of Harringay once more—and there was Billy saying, "You can't leave. We need you. We want Bill out in California to run World Wide Pictures!"

Now I *knew* the Lord was making a big mistake. We had always said that California would be the last place we would want to raise our children, because it seemed there was no really settled family life there. I was rather inclined to agree with Mark Twain who once said, "California is a fine place to live—if you are an orange."

The constant sunshine would be wearisome to this British soul who had been bred on rain and fog! We just felt we would never want to live there permanently. I have learned over the years that you never say *never* when the Lord is directing your life!

I told Billy Graham that Bill was in Plymouth, and he said he would call him there. Many hours of prayer followed. I wondered just what our future held.

When Bill arrived home, I took one look at his eyes and I knew we would be leaving for California very soon. "Goodbye, Plymouth." Goodbye to the old house we had looked at that had a spectacular view of Plymouth Harbor. It was, "Hello, California," and the wretched oranges. I had to make a big adjustment, and I had to make it *fast!*

Bill and I flew out to California; in three days, after looking at so many houses without an ounce of character, we found a little red barn that was a copy of a New England farmhouse. The Lord was giving me a touch of my favorite area of the country, after all. Its beams and brick fireplace mesmerized us, and we fell in love with it immediately. (We were to find it had many flaws, but oh those beams, they kept us looking up!) We flew back to New York to pack our belongings and collect the boys. Moving day came and I thought we would never finish in time. The boys arrived home from school to an empty apartment and found us cleaning up the last-minute mess. When it was time to leave I went into Billy and David's room; and there David sat in a corner, tears rolling down his face as he read a folder of letters his class had written to him. They were farewell letters, and when I started to read them, I sat down with him and bawled too. We prayed together and asked God to bless his friends and thanked Him for them. We asked that He would go before us in our travels to California, and that He would have friends waiting for David there. He was to answer our prayers abundantly.

In all the times of questioning while I packed, there had been two Bible verses which stuck in my mind and would not leave: "And he led them forth by the right way, that they might go to a city of habitation" (Psalms 107:7); and, "...all thy children shall be taught of the Lord; and great shall be the peace of thy children" (Isaiah 54:13). I felt a great peace as we left New York, knowing that God had led us the right way, and that He had promised to take care of our children.

California has proved to be a wonderful home for us. Family life is what you make it, wherever you are. The years we have spent in our house have been exceedingly happy ones, and it has been good to see my children have roots. Of course, there have been the agonies of the teen years—it seems no one can escape their torments. I have always made myself remember what I went through as a teen-ager when I am dealing with many crisis situations. If it were not for the knowledge that I can pour out all my hopes and fears to the Lord on behalf of my children, I know I would have given up years ago. There is a tremendous pull outside the home calling to these adventurous souls; if my knees are calloused, there are very good reasons! Each time our sons leave the house, I try to remember to pray that His loving protection will go with them. They are not perfect, and I would not wish them so, but I am very proud of my two sons who love life and are not afraid to meet it head-on.

Once we were settled in our house, I enjoyed seeing it begin to be a home. Only two months went by and I decided we were indeed "settled." One night I surveyed it lovingly, having spent most of the day polishing the pegged floors until the whole place shone. Bill came home for dinner and remarked how great everything looked.

Next morning at precisely six o'clock we were awakened by a jolting sensation. Our house felt as if it were about to be swept down the hill. A large wall mirror fell down onto our bed (just missing Bill) and the noise of china and glass smashing throughout the house made me realize what we were experiencing. An earthquake! I fought to get out of bed as it rocked convulsively. Then I managed to get to David's room. Bill, Jr., had practically fallen down the stairs from his attic bedroom, and we all huddled, waiting in the hallway to be certain the quake had ended. It was pitch-dark, and no one could find anything when the shaking finally stopped. I could not find a pair of shoes that matched. Bill, Jr., couldn't even find his pants! We were all running around trying to get dressed before another one hit. Finally we got organized, and the morning light began to show us the extent of our damage—$4,500 worth.

The floors I had taken so long to polish were now covered with glass and broken china. Many of my antique plates, which I had brought back from England, were broken and had dug into the boards. Books were everywhere, as the shelves had come down. When I opened the larder where I kept the food, a sight greeted me that was beyond description. Molasses was oozing over all of the debris on the floor. I shut the door and decided to worry about that problem later!

My first reaction was one of thankfulness that not one of us was hurt. We could so easily have been injured. Our house was a mess, but we were untouched. I thanked God. My second reaction was plain annoyance. Here we were supposed to be settled down at last, and now look at this mess. Bill, Jr., was furious, as all of his intricately made models had been broken, and he kept saying, "I'm going to sue. I'm going to sue." When asked just who would be sued, he said he did not know; but he'd find out, and man would he ever sue!

The eeriness that pervaded the area after it was over is something I shall never forget. There was no electricity, no gas, and the water was filled with mud. All over the San Fernando Valley small fires could be seen. I could not help but think of how, at a time like this, we are totally in God's hands, and our only security is in Him. Our lives are always dependent on Him, but sometimes it takes an earthquake to realize how vulnerable we are.

Bill's work now required him to leave us quite often to go with the film crew to different states and countries. I found the separation very hard. Each time I had to pack for him, fears swept over me. Just the sight of that suitcase would send my thoughts racing. "What if something happens to him? I dread the thought of being without him, even for a few weeks!" Then he would be gone, and I would be left with the terrible ache inside me that seemed to drain all my energy.

During a time of separation, I read a letter that Dietrich Bonhoeffer, the theologian, had written while he was imprisoned by the Nazis. In it he told of the unutterable agony of separation, and the longing that was so deep it made him sick. He went on to say:

It is nonsense to say God fills the gap; He does not fill it, but keeps it empty so that our communion with another may be kept alive, even at the cost of pain....The dearer and richer our memories, the more difficult the separation....From the moment we awake until we fall asleep we must commend our loved ones wholly and unreservedly to God, and leave them in His hands, transforming our anxiety for them into prayers on their behalf.

Reading this, I began to realize that all the energy I had exerted, fretting and being concerned, could be turned into a positive force by my prayers. I had prayed for Bill before; but the Lord was showing me that the joys of deeper prayer life with Him could only come about when I turned the ache inside into prayerful attention to the one I loved in Christ.

I began working as a volunteer with wives and mothers of the prisoners of war who were being held in North Vietnam. God used the ache in my heart to help empathize with these courageous women. I could only point them to Jesus as the terrible weeks of waiting turned into years. For some, there was the joy of reunion— for others, the knowledge that their loved one was dead. Yet others had to live with the news that their men were still missing in action.

Recently when Bill and I were discussing with Bill, Jr., his future and our concern for him, he looked us right in the eye and said, "Don't worry about me, Mom and Dad, I know Who I belong to and I know where I'm going." They were words I wish every parent could hear, and we both were so grateful to the Lord for this assurance coming from our son's lips. While attending college, Bill, Jr., has been driving an ambulance. His experiences have made a man out of him in a very few months. One morning he came home after having worked all night (as part of his training) in the emergency room of St. Joseph's Hospital in Burbank. He was weary, but I could tell he did not feel he had worked in vain. Standing with his arms folded over the brick wall that divides our dining room and kitchen, he told me of his experiences. There were so many emergencies that night, but one stood out in his mind above all the others. An epileptic who had tried to commit suicide had been brought to the emergency room. Bill worked on him for hours, holding him when he went into violent fits. During this time, he was able to talk to and comfort this distraught man who felt life was not worth living anymore because of his illness. Bill spoke about the Lord to him, and as the man was wheeled out to be taken to a room in the hospital he said to Bill, Jr., "You've got God in you—don't let anyone take Him away."

After Bill, Jr., finished telling me this story, I thought of the many times when Bill and I had wondered if any of our spiritual training had rubbed off on our children. I was glad some had and was reminded again of Ruth Graham's statement, "You should never judge a painting until the artist is finished with it."

One morning I received a telephone call from Frank Jacobson, vice-president of World Wide Pictures. He and his wife, Dorothy, have been friends of ours ever since we were first married.

"Joan," he said, "how would you like to play Fran Cole, the mother, in *Time to Run?*"

I was speechless as I listened to him telling me that he and Jimmy Collier, who was to direct the film, had been discussing the idea of my playing the part. Naturally I was excited and said that I would love to be able to appear in a film again.

A feeling of joy came over me. I could hardly wait to tell someone. Bill came home for lunch unexpectedly that day, and I raced to the back door to tell him the news.

"Oh, my," he said, "I don't know whether that is a good idea or not. People are going to say it is nepotism—my heading the studios. I shall really have to think about that!"

My balloon was a little deflated but still riding high. Bill, Jr., was next to come home, and when I told him the news he said, "Wow, after all these years of not acting—that may be a real bomb with you in it, Mother!"

Two down and one to go! I was really relying on David to say something positive. I heard him whistling as he came up the hill to our back door, and I hastily opened it and told him the news.

His face lit up, "Congratulations, Mom—let's celebrate!"

Thank You, Lord, for David. He had given me the boost and the assurance I needed.

As the weeks proceeded, the cast and crew were wonderful to me, and I cannot thank the Lord enough for all they came to mean to me. Jimmy Collier gave me the confidence I needed, quietly whispering directions. Randy Carver, who played my son, became like a real son to me. Together with his movie girlfriend, played by Barbara Siegel, we had many enjoyable times. Ed Nelson, whom many remember as Dr. Rossi in *Peyton Place* and who appeared in *Airport '75,* played my husband and proved to be a great help to me. He put so much into his portrayal of a father who was so caught up with his work that he had little time left for his wife and son. Ed told me that if only one life was helped through the movie, he felt it was worth more than anything he had ever done. More than 400,000 decisions for Christ have been made through *Time to Run*.

In preparing for my part, I could only imagine what it would be like if Billy or David had run away from home—the heartache would be unbearable. Fran Cole, the film mother, did not have Christ to help her. I looked at this woman who had nowhere to turn, and I really asked the Lord to help me portray her in such a way that women sitting in the audience could identify with this person.

I toured awhile with the film as it premiered and was overwhelmed many times as I saw God use it. One night I was standing at the back of a theater watching the ending of the film. A teenaged girl spotted me and flung her arms around me, crying. "Thank you, oh, thank you so much—you remind me of my own mother." Then she was gone. I was deeply touched.

My heart has been burdened for today's young people, especially when I read the frightening statistics that coldly announce the numbers who take their own lives. Suicide is the third greatest killer on the college campuses today. "It's empty, life is empty," they cry. If only they could see Jesus wanting to love them, not for what they have achieved, but loving them in the purest sense—unconditionally.

There were many instances of seeing people's gratitude for a film that brought them to Christ. To this day, my Alexandrite ring bears the marks a man made when he shook my hand. He was expressing his thanks for what *Time to Run* had done for his life. While he was telling me that he now understood his responsibility to his son, he did not realize that his hand had grasped mine so tightly that my ring had been crushed. I had it straightened afterwards, but it has never been quite the same. But each time I look at it, I am reminded of a man whose life was changed. Through Christ, he has a deeper understanding of what he should be as a father.

The most meaningful showing of the film, for me, occurred when I was able to go to London with it. Bill and I invited many of the people who had had such an important part in my life. The people attending represented to me a composite of the years that had gone before. There was my Headmistress from school days. She had faithfully taught me the Scriptures and introduced me to Jesus. The same Jesus had to wait for me to follow my heart's desires before I came to a realization that He was all I had been seeking. Joy Elson Rayner, who had been a friend at school, was at the showing. It was she who had dared me to ask for the autograph that led to the beginning of my stage career. Then much later, it was her cousin who had taken me to hear Billy Graham. There were friends from an office where I had worked—dreaming of days ahead that would bring me fame on the stage. Then too, there were many who had helped me in my Christian walk when I needed so much love and understanding. Rose was there. She had been so caught up in the terrible web of drugs when I had first met her. She was hugging me and telling me Jesus was still O.K. as far as she was concerned.

I looked at my family sitting there—my stepmother, Ann, and my sister, Geraldine, my Aunt and Uncle, and my cousin, Audrey, and her husband, John. I remembered the years when they had to watch me go on so blindly. There had been many agonies and very few ecstasies. Now as I spoke to them all, I hoped I could convey my happiness in Christ.

As the film was being shown, I sat there knowing that two other people, with whom I had shared Jesus, could not be there—my father and my grandmother. But they were with Him, and in the darkness of the theater, I was grateful.

In writing, I have had to go back into the past and delve into the recesses of my mind, finding incidents that had long been put aside—hopefully forgotten. It has often been painful. Without

Christ, this would be an empty story of someone still searching, questioning her life. It would be full of meaningless anecdotes, with the heart of it missing.

I have not arrived. There is still so much to learn. By loving Christ and being loved by Him, I am now able to reach out to those who are still seeking and say, "Look what I have found—food for the hunger that gnaws within our souls!"

Our past, our childhood, dominates our future years—how we react to certain situations, our ability to reach out to others. But we cannot lean on our past; we should learn from it, but not let it tear us down. All we confess to the Lord is forgiven and forgotten, just as David said in the Psalms:

> As far as the east is from the west, so far hath he removed our transgressions from us. Like as a father pitieth his children, so the Lord pitieth them that fear him. For he knoweth our frame....
>
> Psalms 103:12-14

Those last five words have been repeated by me, over and over again, when stress has made me feel as if I were going to break again. With a heart cry to God I have thanked Him that He is with me and does know the extent to which this frame can be bent, but not broken. I need to have His resiliency in my life, so that the branches of my mind will not snap, when the times come that make life difficult to bear.

Through understanding the Psalms, we no longer need to feel guilty for all the impassioned feelings that often sweep over us. When David wrote those masterpieces, he was setting a pattern. All who have suffered torments of the mind could look to them and find comfort. He knew the deepest valleys and was not afraid to tell God the truth about himself.

If we were always on a mountaintop, we would miss what God has been able to teach us in the valleys—that He is always with us, even on days when we feel He is unreachable. It is at this time I have to rely completely on my faith and say, "Lord, I do not feel

Your presence with me, but I know that You *are* there, and this wilderness is only temporary in my life."

Moments of doubt have often caused interruption of communication. As if God knew there would be these times, Jesus' encounter with the distraught father, who sought healing for his child in the Gospel of Mark, shows us these are normal feelings:

> Jesus said unto him, If thou canst believe, all things are possible to him that believeth. And straightway the father of the child cried out, and said with tears, Lord, I believe; help thou mine unbelief.
>
> Mark 9:23,24

I have cried out to God my unbelief, and there has always come a peace that is not complacent, but one that is God's. It is not of my own making, for then all I would have in my life would be a feeling of smug satisfaction. I am a weak woman—but I have a strong God.

I was saddened to read a recent statement in a women's magazine by a well-known actress. She said she despised people who crack under strain. Shakespeare put it very succinctly when he said, "He jests at scars that never felt a wound." Those who have never been wounded by the agonies of the mind can never fully understand the tortures that so many go through. But I know this—God understands, for in His life here on earth, Jesus never mocked or belittled those who were weak either in mind or body. He left His scorn for those who felt themselves better than others.

We are all made differently. We are all born with a distinct personality. No two fingerprints are alike, and this is what comforts me. It makes me realize that a God who has taken the time to attend to these minute details, cares deeply for the individual He has created. He cares for all the happenings in our lives, however small or insignificant.

Some time ago, during a visit to a jail in Honolulu where I was allowed to talk to some of the girls, I met a young prisoner whose eyes showed she was scared to death. She had come into the room in her shapeless prison dress, thongs that did not fit properly on her feet, and smoking a cigarette. She sat down and seemed unapproachable.

A few scenes from *Time to Run* were shown, and then I spoke briefly about the forgiveness of Christ in my life. I told of the love that was waiting if only we would receive it. Then I asked if we could pray together.

When I looked up, the girl with the scared eyes was crying.

"Pat," I said, "can I help you in any way?"

"No, there's no hope for me. I've known about God, but I have failed Him so terribly. There's nothing anyone can do."

Gradually she told me this story. She was the granddaughter of a minister, and she knew all about the Bible. But she felt there was no forgiveness left for her. I turned to 1 John 1:9, and quickly she said, "I know that verse—that won't help me!"

But I read it to her anyway. "If we confess our sins, he is faithful and just to forgive us our sins, and to cleanse us from all unrighteousness."

"Pat, don't you see God is saying He will forgive *all* unrighteousness?"

She looked at the verse, then up at me. "I've never thought about that word *all*."

We talked for a while, and I began to see a change in her face when she realized there was still hope for her. *All* unrighteousness meant *every* unrighteousness. She prayed with me that Christ would come in and forgive everything in her life. As she looked up, there were still tears in her eyes, but this time I could see she had reached out and grasped hope from our Saviour.

Pat still had to face trial, possible extradition, and a long separation from her little girl whom she adored. We hugged as I left, and I promised to keep in touch with her. Next day I was allowed to telephone the jail to find out how she was. She told me that Jesus had been so real to her, and no matter what she had to face now, she knew she would not be alone.

Over the months I wrote to her and received the most wonderful letters. She was extradited to the mainland and was sentenced to serve two years in the Women's Penitentiary. She knew she had to pay for her crime and accepted her sentence, bearing the heartache of being parted from her little girl. Her letters arrived regularly and they were always filled with words of belief in God's love for her. One letter told of an incident that had distressed her. It was rough there. A matron had bleach thrown in her face and was blinded. Pat had her ups and downs, but she was hanging on tight to Christ. She looked forward to being free and providing a Christian home for her daughter.

Pat helped others in the penitentiary to find Christ, and even when her first parole request was turned down, she took it bravely.

The same day I signed the contract with Fleming H. Revell to write this book, I received a letter from Pat. It contained the news both of us had been praying for: She was *free* and wanted to tell *everyone!*

To this day, I do not know what her crime was. I never asked. I only saw her as a person, like myself, who needed the forgiveness of Christ and the hope that He alone could give.

This is the reason I have wanted to write this book. Like Pat I want to tell everyone that I, too, am free! Free from the prison that had invisible bars, for it was a prison within my mind and soul. Jesus said, "If the Son therefore shall make you free, ye shall be free indeed" (John 8:36).

We make our own prisons when we shut out God. I am no longer bound, but free—free to worship Him. There are days when I feel I can reach out and touch the very heights of heaven, as I find such consolation in the knowledge of His love.

Among my memorabilia is a letter that has meant a great deal to me. It is dated September 25, 1957, and was written by Mrs. J. Edwin Orr, Port Shepstone, South Africa, to Mrs. Ruth Graham. Here is an excerpt from it:

> You know when Edwin was in a very remote part of New South Wales, more than 500 miles from Sydney, a man approached him. He told Edwin an amazing story and I knew you'd be interested.

He said he'd been looking at an Australian picture magazine more than four years before and his eye was attracted to a photo of an actress. Having nothing to do with the movies, he was not impressed, but a strange conviction from the Spirit burdened him to pray for her conversion. He personally felt it was a waste of time, nevertheless, he kept praying for the girl. In 1954, the burden lifted, as if the Lord said, "You need not carry this burden any longer." He had no idea whether the girl died or was truly converted....But he remembered her name— Joan Winmill—and when Edwin checked dates with him he found that the burden had lifted during the Harringay Crusade, when you were actually helping Joan! The man's name is Ellwood Fischer and he is a great man of prayer. Naturally, he was greatly encouraged to learn of Joan Winmill's conversion. Knowing that you must be in touch with Joan, I thought you might wish to tell her how a stranger in far-off Australia prayed so long for her conversion.

If I ever needed proof that God answers prayers, this letter is emblazoned on my heart as evidence. While I was alone without hope in the apartment in London, crying out to Him, a man many thousands of miles away in Australia was touched by the Spirit to pray for me.

I will praise the Lord no matter what happens. I will constantly speak of his glories and grace. I will boast of all his kindness to me. Let all who are discouraged take heart. Let us praise the Lord together, and exalt his name.

For I cried to him and he answered me! He freed me from all my fears.

Psalms 34:1-4, LB

A Special Word from Billy Graham on Loneliness

> And ye shall seek me, and find me, when ye shall search
> for me with all your heart.
>
> Jeremiah 29:13

You started on the Great Quest the moment you were born. It
was many years perhaps before you realized it, before it became
apparent that you were constantly searching—searching for something you never had—searching for something that was more important than anything in life. Sometimes you have tried to forget
about it. Sometimes you have attempted to lose yourself in other
things, so there could be time and thought for nothing but the business at hand. Sometimes you may even have felt that you were
freed from the need to go on seeking this nameless thing. At moments you have almost been able to dismiss the quest completely.
But always you have been caught up in it again—always you have
had to come back to your search.

At the loneliest moments in your life, you have looked at other
men and women and wondered if they too were seeking—seeking
something they couldn't describe but knew they wanted and
needed. Some of them seemed so much happier and less burdened
than you. Some of them seemed to have found fulfillment in marriage and family living. Others went off to achieve fame and wealth
in other parts of the world. Still others stayed at home and pros-
pered. Looking at them you may have thought: "These people are
not on the Great Quest. These people have found their way. They
knew what they wanted and have been able to grasp it. It is only I
who travel this path that leads to nowhere. It is only I who go ask-

ing, seeking, stumbling along this dark and despairing road that has no guideposts.''

But you are not alone. All mankind is traveling with you, for all mankind is on this same quest. All humanity is seeking the answer to the confusion, the moral sickness, the spiritual emptiness that oppresses the world. All mankind is crying out for guidance, for comfort, for peace.

We don't know what it is. It makes us restless. You see, man was made for God; and without God, he is lonely.

After the death of her husband, Queen Victoria said, ''There is no one left to call me Victoria.'' Even though she was a queen, she knew what it meant to be lonely.

Loneliness is no respecter of persons. It invades the palace as well as the hut. Many turn to drink because of it. Others lose their sanity. Thousands have found Christ to be the answer for their loneliness.

As Rupert Brooke was sailing from Liverpool to New York, he was overcome with a feeling of loneliness because all the other passengers had friends to bid them farewell. Then he noticed a little dirty-faced boy on the wharf. He rushed down and said, ''Young man, do you want to earn some money?''

The little fellow nodded yes.

''Then wave to me when the boat leaves,'' Brooke said.

Modern writers depict the pessimism of our time and many of them throw up their hands in despair and say, ''There is no answer to man's dilemma.'' Hemingway once said, ''I live in a vacuum that is as lonely as a radio tube when the batteries are dead, and there is no current to plug into.'' Eugene O'Neill in ''Long Day's Journey Into Night'' typifies the philosophical attitude of our day. He says, ''Life's only meaning is death.'' I say to Hemingway and O'Neill, who have already gone on, ''There is more to life than death.'' There is more to life than a radio tube that needs a place to plug into. Jesus taught us the dignity and importance of being a person. God put us on this earth for a purpose, and our purpose is fellowship with God and to glorify God.

If you are lonely today I beg you, come to Christ and know the fellowship that He gives.

Some people think success or money or material things will bring them happiness, but deep in their hearts they know the truth of God's Word. They know that their glamorous, successful lives are just a front for an aching emptiness within. The Bible says, "What shall it profit a man if he should gain the whole world and lose his own soul?"

There may even be those reading this who believe that suicide will provide the answer to all their problems, but God's Word makes it clear you can't run away from your problems, in this life or the next. But if you come to the foot of the Cross of Jesus, and admit that you need forgiveness, you can find the "peace that passes understanding."

Fifth, there is the LONELINESS OF SIN. There are thousands of lonely people in the city and in the country, who carry heavy and difficult burdens of grief, anxiety, pain and disappointment; but the loneliest soul of all is the man whose life is steeped in sin.

Christ can give you power to overcome every sin and habit in your life. He can break the ropes, fetters, and chains of sin.

Perhaps you have at one time known the joy and peace of being born into God's family. You knew the sweet fellowship of God's people. You knew the complete happiness and satisfaction of Christ's presence with you, but you sinned. You went out from the presence of Christ, and you have found that it is night. You have neither the fellowship of Christians nor the fellowship of sinners, and certainly you no longer have the fellowship of Christ. Perhaps there is no loneliness quite so bitter as the loneliness of a backslidden Christian.

Yet there is forgiveness for you. As you confess and forsake your sins, your fellowship with Christ will be restored. "If we confess our sins, he is faithful and just to forgive us our sins, and to cleanse us from all unrighteousness" (1 John 1:9).

Last, there is the LONELINESS OF THE SAVIOR. Jesus knows what it is to be alone. On the Cross, He cried out, "My God, my God, why hast thou forsaken me?" Not only had He been forsaken by His human companions, but now in that desperate hour, He, because He was bearing our sin in His own body, was alone.

And in dying on the Cross He took your sin and your judgment. And now God says, "I will meet you at the Cross; I won't meet you anywhere else, but I will meet you at the Cross. If you will come in repentance of sin and by faith, I will meet you at the Cross of my Son, Jesus Christ." Jesus said, "I am the way, the truth and the life."

The Bible says that repentance of sin and coming by faith to submit and surrender your life to Jesus Christ is an act of commitment. It is a choice. It is a surrender in which you surrender yourself--everything you have--to Jesus Christ as Lord and Savior. In the quietness of your heart you can know Christ now.

Whether you are rich or poor, whatever your background may be, whatever your needs are, you can be a changed person, a transformed person having eternal life, if you are ready to bend your will to the will of God, if you are ready to renounce your sin, and if you are ready by faith to receive Christ as your Savior.

When Joan Winmill came to Christ during that crusade in Harringay Arena, she experienced the deep peace that only Jesus Christ can give. Hers was a tortuous path to the Cross, but the healing presence of the Savior has sustained her these many years.

All human need can be met at the Cross of Christ. Your need may not be exactly the same as Joan Winmill's, but Jesus Christ is still active in the world; and His Spirit is still able to ease the pain of human experience and sin in the heart and life of anyone who will openly seek Him.

It is my prayer that you will come to Christ if you have not already done so. When Joan Winmill came forward in our meetings she was given Bible study material and aids that helped her to become familiar with God's Word. We will be happy to send you similar material absolutely free of charge, if you would write to me. When you write, let us know that you are receiving Jesus Christ, so that we might be better able to pray for you.

Billy Graham Evangelistic Association
Box 779, Minneapolis, Minnesota 55440